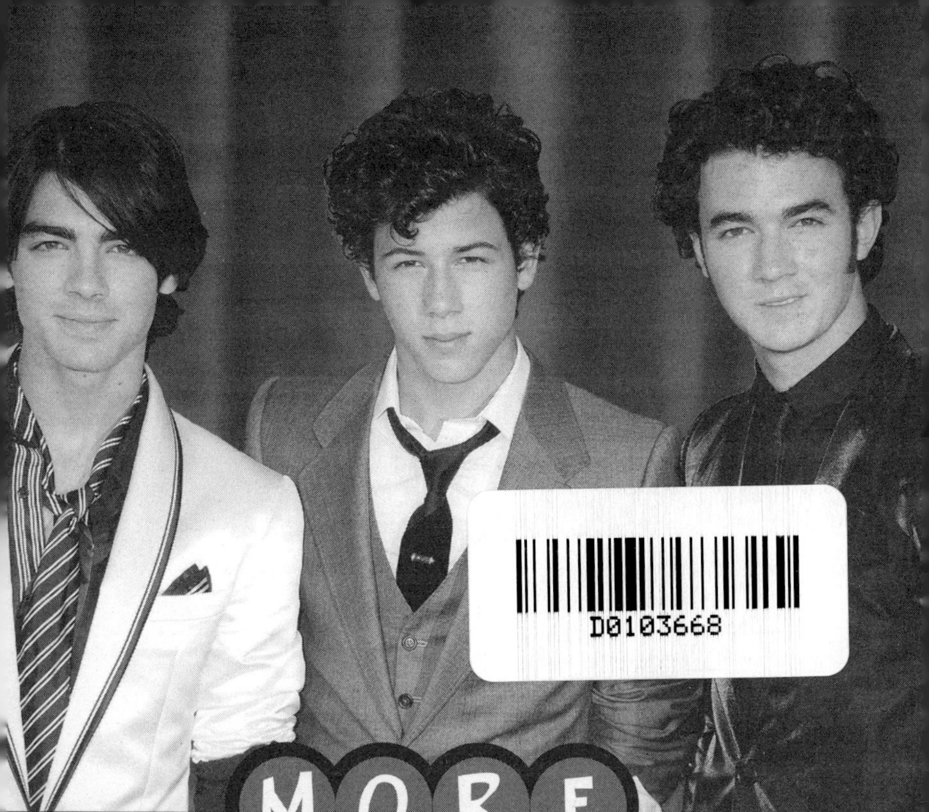

MORE JAMMIN' WITH THE JONAS BROTHERS

AN UNAUTHORIZED BIOGRAPHY BY LEXI RYALS

PSS!
PRICE STERN SLOAN

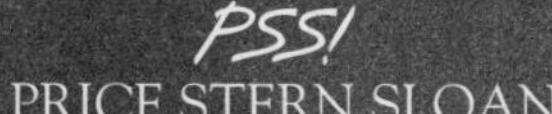

PRICE STERN SLOAN
Published by the Penguin Group
Penguin Group (USA) Inc., 375 Hudson Street, New York, New York 10014, USA
Penguin Group (Canada), 90 Eglinton Avenue East, Suite 700, Toronto, Ontario M4P 2Y3, Canada
(a division of Pearson Penguin Canada Inc.)
Penguin Books Ltd., 80 Strand, London WC2R 0RL, England
Penguin Group Ireland, 25 St. Stephen's Green, Dublin 2, Ireland
(a division of Penguin Books Ltd.)
Penguin Group (Australia), 250 Camberwell Road, Camberwell, Victoria 3124, Australia
(a division of Pearson Australia Group Pty. Ltd.)
Penguin Books India Pvt. Ltd., 11 Community Centre, Panchsheel Park, New Delhi—110 017, India
Penguin Group (NZ), 67 Apollo Drive, Rosedale, North Shore 0632, New Zealand
(a division of Pearson New Zealand Ltd.)
Penguin Books (South Africa) (Pty.) Ltd., 24 Sturdee Avenue, Rosebank, Johannesburg 2196, South Africa

Penguin Books Ltd., Registered Offices: 80 Strand, London WC2R 0RL, England

Photo credits: Cover: Bob Charlotte/PR Photo; Insert photos: first page courtesy of Kevin Winter/Getty Images; second page courtesy of Lester Cohen/WireImage, Brad Barket/Getty Images; third page courtesy of Scott Gries/Getty Images; fourth page courtesy of Dave M. Benett/Getty Images, Frank Micelotta/Getty Images for MTV; fifth page courtesy of Scott Gries/Getty Images, Brendan Hoffman/Getty Images; sixth page courtesy of James Devaney/WireImage; seventh page courtesy of Scott Gries/Getty Images, Frank Micelotta/TCA 2008/Getty Images for Fox; eighth page courtesy of Kevin Winter/TCA 2008/Getty Images for Fox

Library of Congress Control Number: 2008046098

ISBN 978-0-8431-8929-2

10 9 8 7 6 5 4 3 2 1

CONTENTS

INTRODUCTION

LOVEBUG

The annual Video Music Awards on MTV is the hottest music awards show for the most current names in music. Every performance at the awards is a showstopper, and the September 7, 2008, show was no exception. There were performances from big names like Rihanna, Lil Wayne, Paramore, T.I., Christina Aguilera, Kid Rock, Kanye West, and Pink. But the most highly anticipated performance of the night was, by far, from the Jonas Brothers.

Kevin, Joe, and Nick Jonas were nominated for Best Pop Video and Video of the Year that night, but fans were more interested in seeing the hard-rockin' trio perform one of the songs from their recently released album *A Little Bit Longer*. No one in the crowd knew what the Jonas boys had planned for their number, but everyone knew it was going to be big. A clock even ran along the bottom of the screen, counting down the minutes and seconds until the Jonas Brothers' big number.

When the brothers' close friend Taylor Swift took the stage to introduce Kevin, Joe, and Nick, the crowd went absolutely wild. A huge screen on the stage showed one of the back lots at Paramount Studios that is set up to look exactly like the streets of New York City. Joe got out of a cab and joined Kevin and Nick to sit on a stoop wearing old-fashioned trousers, button-downs, vests, and suspenders. Kevin and Nick had their guitars in hand and Joe was holding a microphone and a tambourine. As soon as Joe sat down, the boys started off with what appeared to be an acoustic version of their single "Lovebug."

Then, midway through the song, the boys turned up the heat! Buildings behind them pulled away to reveal their backup band and hundreds of screaming fans poured onto the set to surround the newly revealed stage. The boys pulled out their electric guitars to finish the song. There were girls on every side of the stage. They were screaming, crying, and dancing with all of their hearts. And who can blame them? They were watching their all-time favorite band perform for one of the biggest music award shows of 2008!

Kevin, Joe, and Nick were stunned by the response to their performance, as Kevin explained to People.com. "It's pretty amazing. You grow up watching the VMAs. You know the performances; you see the pictures in every magazine."

That night was a dream come true for the Jonas Brothers. In the year leading up to the VMAs, the boys had released their first critically acclaimed number 1 album, sold out almost every single venue of their first tour as headliners, starred in a hit made-for-television movie, and, most importantly, proved that they have what it takes to have a long-term successful career. And, if their VMAs performance is any indication of what's to come, the Jonas Brothers are just getting warmed up!

CHAPTER 1
JOINING THE JONAS FAMILY

It's really no surprise that the Jonas boys are such skilled and talented musicians. When Paul Kevin Jonas Sr. (he goes by Kevin Sr.) married Denise right after they graduated from college, they were both musicians who had dedicated their lives to spreading the message of Christianity. They met at Christ for the Nations Bible College in Dallas, Texas. Christ for the Nations is a ministry school that was founded in 1970. More than 28,000 students have graduated from the institute and have gone on to dedicate their lives to evangelical work. After school, the young couple settled in Dallas and continued to work with Christ for the Nations. Denise was proficient in sign language, and she and her husband traveled across the country, leading worship programs for the hearing impaired.

The Jonases loved their work, but Denise and Kevin Sr. wanted to start a family. On November 5, 1987, they welcomed their first son, Paul Kevin Jonas II, into the world. The new parents decided to call their little one Kevin. Shortly after Kevin was born, the Jonas family went back on the road to continue spreading the Christian message. Kevin was a very easygoing baby and he loved traveling with his parents. But Kevin wasn't alone for long; less than two years later he became a big brother.

Kevin Sr. and Denise were working in sunny Arizona on August 15, 1989, when Denise gave birth to her second son. The proud parents named their new arrival Joseph Adam Jonas, or Joe for short. As Kevin and Joe grew a little older, Denise and Kevin Sr. had their hands full with the two rambunctious toddlers. Kevin was a thoughtful child, but Joe's sense of adventure would later earn him the nickname "Danger."

The two boys had big imaginations. Kevin had decided early on what his future profession would be: a cowboy or, if that fell through, an astronaut. So Kevin and Joseph often pretended to be cowboys in the Old West or astronauts and aliens flying through space. But Joe actually wanted to be a comedian one day. He was a silly child who was full of energy and loved telling jokes. Together, the pair certainly kept their parents on their toes!

With two young children, the Jonas family decided to take a break from traveling when Kevin Sr. was offered a job as the worship leader at Christ for the Nations Music. Kevin Sr. led worship services, taught music students at the institute, and worked on his own music. Kevin Sr. also wrote several songs that became popular in churches across the country.

Kevin made friends right away in Dallas, but Joe was a little bit shy and took longer to open up. The two continued to be inseparable, and they spent a lot of time running around Christ for the Nations and listening in on their parents' music projects. Things changed again when Denise announced that she was pregnant shortly after the family got settled into their new home. Nine months later, on September 16, 1992, Nicholas Jerry Jonas was born.

Nick had a distinctive personality right from the start. As soon as he could talk, Nick began singing, and he was a natural-born performer. When he was only two years old, he used his grandmother's turkey baster as a microphone and a coffee table as a stage for his performances. When his grandmother tried to get Nick down off the table, he replied, "No, I need to practice. I'm going to be on Broadway."

When he wasn't practicing his performance skills, quiet, shy Nick loved to tag along after his older brothers. Like all brothers, they had fights over silly little things, but for the most part they loved spending time together.

In 1996, the family moved again, this time to Wyckoff, New Jersey. Kevin Sr. took a job as the senior pastor at the Wyckoff Assembly of God Church and the family moved into a split-level redbrick house nearby. Most kids would have been heartbroken to be torn away from their school and friends, but not the Jonas boys. As Kevin explained to *Cross Rhythms*, "I only really had one big transition and that was in third grade. I went from Dallas to New Jersey. Other than that I only switched schools after middle school and going to high school. So it was never really that big of a deal to me."

Kevin, Joe, and Nick fit right in in New Jersey. Wyckoff is about twenty-five miles outside of New York City, so the move opened up a world of culture to the young children. The family took plenty of trips into Manhattan to visit museums, see Broadway shows, and play in Central Park. Nick was especially inspired by New York City's theater scene. "I've been performing since I was like 3 and singing since I was 2," Nick told the *New York Times*. "I'd watch *Peter Pan*, the VHS of the Broadway version, and I'd have a temper tantrum if anybody turned it off." *Peter Pan* was his favorite musical in those days. "I would watch every single movement—the dancing, how they acted, how their mouths moved when they sang," Nick explained to *Clubhouse*.

Kevin, Nick, and Joseph loved swimming and riding their bikes in their new neighborhood, and their proud parents took plenty of pictures of their boys! The brothers also enjoyed sports, video games, reading books, and watching cartoons. Nick especially loved *Batman*, as he told *People*. "[I] had this Batman costume that I wore all the time. It was awesome. I would run around in my backyard and be Batman." Some of their other favorite cartoons were *Veggie Tales* and Nickelodeon's *Blue's Clues*. Joseph even dressed up as Blue from *Blue's Clues* and Nick as Bob from *Veggie Tales* for Halloween one year! (Kevin went as Cavity Sam from the Milton Bradley game Operation.) Their other favorite shows were Nickelodeon's *All That* and, of course, anything on the Disney Channel!

The brothers were enrolled in Eastern Christian School, a private pre-K–12 preparatory school, and all three of them did well in their classes. The small classes and dedication to Christian values appealed to Kevin Sr. and Denise, and the boys made some great friends there. Kevin was in third grade, Joseph was in second grade, and Nick started kindergarten there.

Denise and Kevin Sr. were also adamant that music be a big part of their boys' lives. "We kind of always grew up into music and making music with my dad," Joe told the *Houston Chronicle*. "He was part of record labels and things like that. My mom's an amazing singer. We kind of grew into it." The boys got their ear for catchy music from their dad. The Jonases raised their boys on James Taylor and Carole King, and Kevin Sr. followed the careers of music producers closely. "We'd have friends over, and we'd be listening to the new Backstreet Boys CD, and he'd talk about how amazing Max Martin was," Nick told *Rolling Stone*, referring to the Swedish boy-band producer.

The Jonas boys learned to play piano, and the family often had sing-alongs in the evenings. But Kevin amped up the boys' musical involvement when he taught himself how to play guitar at eleven years old. He was at home sick from school one day, and he was really bored. So he picked up one of his dad's guitars, found a book on guitar basics, and spent the rest of the day learning the main chords. Kevin was hooked immediately. He even pretended to be sick for another two days so he could stay home and play! Kevin is a perfectionist, so he spent all of his spare time practicing until he could play like an expert. He then taught both of his brothers how to play so that they could jam together. After that, Nick learned how to play drums so that he could keep the rhythm.

The Jonas boys spent a lot of time at church since their dad was the senior pastor. It had always been a big part of their lives, but as they grew older, they each made personal decisions to be Christians. The whole family was involved in church programs.

Kevin Sr. worked to build up the church's outreach and music programs and continued to travel to other congregations to aid with their worship. Denise kept busy working with the hearing impaired. Kevin, Nick, and Joe were very involved in outreach programs, Bible studies, and worship services. On Sundays, the brothers would watch their dad deliver his sermon and play songs on his guitar. Kevin, Joe, and Nick would sing, too. "We grew up in church, playing with our father onstage," Kevin told *Rolling Stone*. As soon as Nick was old enough, he joined the church's children's choir—he even sang with the adult choir a few times! And his soulful voice caught everyone's attention.

When Nick was only six years old, he got even more into performing. He started a drama group called the Radicals at church. Nick and his friends would put on skits based on Bible stories for the younger kids. The Radicals are still active at the Assembly of God and perform six outreach programs a year.

The brothers were very proud of their parents' work, as Nick explained to *Cross Rhythms*. "They started a sign language ministry . . . They went all over the world. It was pretty amazing. They stopped when I was born, which was thirteen years ago. Then my dad became the senior pastor at the church in Wyckoff, New Jersey, when we moved there. It was just amazing how the Lord planned it all. We moved to New Jersey and right there is where everything happens in the music industry and it kind of all came into place. It was really cool."

The Jonas family was very happy in New Jersey. Kevin Sr. and Denise's work was going well, and the boys were excelling at their new school. Little did they know that stardom was waiting right around the corner, and it all started with a haircut . . .

CHAPTER 2

BROADWAY, HERE THEY COME!

Nick was a born songbird. He sang everywhere—in the shower, on the street, and even at the local salon! Before Nick was in school full-time with his older brothers, Denise used to take Nick with her to get her hair done at the salon. Nick would walk up and down in front of the mirrors belting out pop songs and show tunes. The other women in the salon would often pay him for his performances with candy money. Luckily for all of the Jonas Brothers' fans, one of the women who visited the salon regularly had a son who performed on Broadway. She was so impressed with little Nick's big voice that she approached Denise about him. "She said, 'Do you have a manager?'" Kevin Sr. told *Rolling Stone*. "She said, 'He needs a manager, because my son did this, and he can do this.'" She urged Denise to call a talent agent in Manhattan named Shirley Grant.

For days, Nick begged his mother to let him meet the talent agent—he had been dreaming about starring on Broadway since he was two, after all! His parents finally gave in, and Kevin Sr. and Denise took Nick into Manhattan to audition for Shirley. Nick was always a little shy about meeting new people, but as soon as he started singing, all of his shyness melted away. After Nick sang a few songs, Shirley could tell he was a born performer. She offered to represent Nick, and the Jonases accepted. Nick was on his way to becoming a star!

Nick must have been thrilled to have an agent. She told him to practice performing, but Nick already had plenty of practice belting out tunes in his living room. "From the time I was two years old, I would wake up in the morning and start singing all the time, every second of the day," Nick told

MusicRemedy.com. Even so, Nick probably still spent a lot of time practicing. Shirley sent him on auditions for commercials, recordings, and plays and musicals on and off Broadway.

Nicholas loved going to all types of auditions, but he was determined to land a role on Broadway. "[F]rom whenever I can remember, I've been telling my grandma I was going to be on Broadway," he told *TeenStar*. Most casting agents had probably never seen such a young actor with so much ambition! Nick's parents made sure that Nick only auditioned for roles that they felt were appropriate. "I really observed the other parents," Denise told *Rolling Stone*. "I thought, 'I'm a novice, and I don't want to make any mistakes that could be detrimental to us as a family or their careers down the road.' We weighed *everything*. Sometimes they'd throw a script at us that was full of language not suitable for a seven-year-old."

And Denise really did have to watch out because Nick became popular very quickly. He immediately began landing roles and was soon in high demand. He sang backup vocals on recordings, had bit parts in commercials, and performed in a number of off-Broadway productions in New Jersey and New York. And he wasn't the only one! Kevin and Joseph signed on with Shirley, too, and they landed roles over the next six years as extras alongside their youngest brother in commercials for Clorox, Burger King, LEGO, Chuck E. Cheese, BattleBots, and the Disney Channel, just to name a few. The boys must have loved being on set together, especially while filming toy and food commercials. After all, who wouldn't love to get paid to play with cool toys and eat delicious burgers and pizza?

Nick was only seven when he took his first step toward the bright lights of Broadway. He was chosen to play the roles of Tiny Tim and Young Scrooge in *A Christmas Carol: The Musical* at Madison Square Garden. *A Christmas Carol: The Musical* was the first Broadway-style production to be staged at the WaMu

Theater in Madison Square Garden. It ran from 1994 until 2004 and was choreographed and directed by Tony Award winner Susan Stroman. In those ten years, over 2.5 million people saw the show. Nick was a part of the cast for the 1999 holiday season.

A Christmas Carol is one of the most famous holiday stories of all time. It was written by Charles Dickens in 1843 and tells the story of a miserable, rich old man named Ebenezer Scrooge, who hates Christmas and only cares about making money. Then, one Christmas Eve, Scrooge is visited by the Ghosts of Christmas Past, Christmas Present, and Christmas Yet to Come. The three ghosts show him error of his ways. By the next morning, Christmas Day, Scrooge is a changed man and sets about righting his many wrongs. This little story has impacted millions of people over the years and has become synonymous with the hopeful spirit of the holiday season.

Tiny Tim is the youngest son of Scrooge's clerk, Bob Cratchit. Scrooge barely pays Cratchit enough to feed his family. Tiny Tim is sick and crippled, but he is full of faith. It is Tiny Tim's plight that makes Scrooge eventually see how wrong his penny-pinching, greedy ways are. It was a lot of responsibility for Nick to take on such a pivotal role. He even got to say one of the most famous lines in the entire play, "God bless us, every one." Nick wasn't a bit nervous—okay, maybe just a bit—but he was extremely excited.

In addition to Tiny Tim, Nick played a younger version of Scrooge in several scenes when the Ghost of Christmas Past visits Scrooge. Playing dual roles certainly kept Nick hopping backstage, but he loved every minute of it. His big voice filled the theater night after night as he belted out classic Christmas carols. Nick was busy every minute of that holiday season, but a lead role in one of the biggest shows in Manhattan was the best Christmas present he could have asked for. Nick did manage to keep a full workload at school, only missing Wednesdays for matinee performances. Nick's dad drove him into the city every day and watched every performance and rehearsal. During the long car rides, Kevin Sr. and Nick talked about music nonstop. "All the way home and back, we'd write songs," Kevin Sr. told *Rolling Stone*.

Nick caught the eye of several Broadway heavyweights during his run in *A Christmas Carol*, and in 2001 he landed his first role on Broadway. Nick played Little Jake in Irving Berlin's *Annie Get Your Gun* opposite Crystal Bernard and country music star Reba McEntire. *Annie Get Your Gun* is the story of sharpshooter Annie Oakley's romance with Frank Butler. It was originally produced by the famous Richard Rogers and Oscar Hammerstein II in 1946, and featured the now-classic Broadway songs "Anything You Can Do" and "There's No Business Like Show Business." The revival that Nick appeared in opened on Broadway in February 1999 at the Marquis Theatre and won the 1999 Tony Award for Best Revival of a Musical.

Nick's big moment in the musical occurred

when his character sings "Doin' What Comes Natur'lly" with Annie. Annie is haggling with a shopkeeper and admits that she hasn't had much of an education. She then bursts into song about how some things can't be taught. Nick and several other young children join in during the chorus. Little Nick looked adorable dressed in a brown leather jacket and pants and a coonskin cap. His booming voice and ability to quickly pick up choreography really set him apart from the other child actors. And his experiences in *Annie Get Your Gun* certainly came in handy in his next role as the adorable little teacup Chip in *Beauty and the Beast*.

Nick was nine years old when he joined the cast of *Beauty and the Beast* on Broadway. He performed as Chip every Wednesday evening, Friday evening, Saturday afternoon, and Sunday evening for six months. *Beauty and the Beast* enjoyed a thirteen-year run on Broadway from 1994 to 2007. It is based on the Disney animated feature film of the same name that premiered in 1991 and tells the classic French fairy tale "Beauty and the Beast" with a Disney twist.

The musical follows the story of Belle, a beautiful and intelligent French girl, and the Beast, a cursed prince. Belle discovers that all of the household objects in the Beast's castle are alive, the victims of an enchantment. What Belle doesn't know is that the Beast must find a woman to love who loves him in return before an enchanted rose dies to break the curse. All of the household items in the palace are actually the palace's staff. They work to get Belle and the Beast to fall in love, and eventually it works. But their happy ending is almost ruined when the townspeople of Belle's village attack the castle and try to kill the Beast. However, Belle arrives in time to tell the Beast that she loves him, and he and the palace staff are returned to their former selves. Then Belle and the Beast are married and live happily ever after.

Chip, the part Nick played, is the adorable teacup son of Mrs. Potts, the head housekeeper who was transformed into a teapot. The role called for a young actor with a resounding tenor voice, great comedic timing, and a lovable smile—naturally, Nick was a perfect fit. It was a much bigger role than his part in *Annie Get Your Gun*, and Nick was very excited for the chance to really show off his acting chops. His vocals were featured in the songs "Be Our Guest," "Human Again," "The Battle," and the reprise of "Beauty and the Beast." He also got to wear a fun teacup costume that fitted down over his shoulders and ride around in a special cart for portions of the play. Nick loved playing Chip and was very excited when the producers wanted him to sign on for another six months, but another opportunity came along that Nick just couldn't turn down.

A few weeks before Nick was going to sign his new *Beauty and the Beast* contract, Nick got some incredible news. He was invited to join the Tony Award-winning cast of *Les Misérables* in the role of Gavroche. "I was at Bible camp," Nick told *Clubhouse*, "and I felt God saying, 'You're going to be in *Les Misérables* and touch many people.'" So Nick let another actor take the role of Chip and he happily joined the final cast of *Les Misérables*.

Les Misérables, or "Les Miz," as fans affectionately call it, is an emotionally charged musical set in Paris during the French Revolution. It is an adaptation of Victor Hugo's 1862 novel of the same name, and tells the story of an ex-convict who finds redemption by living a just and good life. The role of Gavroche was the biggest role Nicholas had ever played. He had many lines, a solo song, and a dramatic death scene, but Nick was ready for the challenge. He worked harder than he had ever worked for a show and wowed critics with his performance. Being a principal member of a Broadway cast has its advantages, and Nick was proud to be part of such a distinguished community. "It's awesome; I love everything about it," Nick told *Clubhouse*. "It's so exciting to go onstage every day—to sing a song and know 1,500 people are watching!"

Nick was the first Jonas brother to make it to the Broadway stage, but he wasn't the only one. Joe had appeared in several commercials with Nick, but he was focused on becoming a comedian until he tagged along with Nick on one of his auditions. Nicholas was auditioning for a role in the musical *Oliver*, and the producers were very impressed with his look, amazing voice, and professionalism, but Nick was too small for the role. They jokingly asked if he had any brothers, and Nick answered very seriously that he did, in fact, have a brother named Joseph who was waiting out in the hall. The producers asked Joe to come in. They liked his look as well and asked him to return the next day for his own audition. "I didn't know what to expect," Joseph told the *Kansas City Star.* "I went home and learned the song that night and I was like I'm not going to sing! I already have my guitar." But Joe rocked the audition and was cast as one of the orphans in the musical. It was the start of Joe's Broadway career. "I have been in several Broadway plays, including *La Bohème*, *The Velveteen Rabbit*, and *Oliver*," Joe told *Teen* magazine.

Oliver is the musical version of Charles Dickens's classic novel about an orphan boy on the streets of London. In the story, Oliver runs away from his orphanage and is taken in by the Artful Dodger and his band of pickpockets. When Oliver goes on his first mission, he gets caught by a rich, kindly old man. The old man takes Oliver home, but Oliver is kidnapped by the old orphanage owners when they discover he may have come from a wealthy family. Eventually, the Artful Dodger rescues Oliver and returns him to the kindly old man and they discover that Oliver is actually the old man's grandson. The show required lots of singing and dancing, and Joe had a great time working on his first musical—especially since he got to use a British accent. Joe has always loved accents!

The next show Joe had a role in was an off-Broadway production of *The Velveteen Rabbit*. It is the story of a beloved toy rabbit that belongs to a little boy. The little boy loves the rabbit very much, but when he becomes sick, the rabbit is taken away because it might have germs. But because the boy loved the rabbit so much, the Nursery Magic Fairy comes and makes the rabbit real. The sweet and touching story has been a favorite of children everywhere, and it was always a favorite of the Jonas boys. Joe had a lot of fun performing in a show just for kids!

Then, in 2002, Joseph landed a role in one of the most talked-about musicals of the year, Baz Luhrmann's *La Bohème*. *La Bohème* ran from December 8, 2002, through June 29, 2003, at the Broadway Theatre. Baz Luhrmann is the critically acclaimed director of the films *Romeo + Juliet* and *Moulin Rouge*. When he decided to bring Puccini's classic opera *La Bohème* to Broadway, the theater world took notice. He decided to relocate the story from 1840s Paris to the Left Bank of Paris in 1957.

Luhrmann billed *La Bohème* as "the greatest

love story ever sung." Giacomo Puccini originally wrote the opera in 1896. It is the story of several poor artists living in Paris and their struggles to find love and overcome poverty and disease. *La Bohème* is ultimately a tragic love story that has resonated with people from all walks of life since its debut. It has been performed in almost every opera house in the world and has been adapted again and again to appeal to new generations.

Joseph performed with the children's chorus and learned a lot about showmanship from Baz Luhrmann. "That was pretty amazing. It was a great experience. I think it was really preparing me for what I'm doing today. You know, discipline and all that stuff that's needed for what you're doing in the music industry. I loved the experience," Joe told *Cross Rhythms*. The show was nominated for six Tony Awards during its run.

The Jonas boys had become some of the most in-demand child stars on Broadway. And Joe and Nick both loved the thrill of performing in front of packed houses every night. "People always used to imply, 'Are you concerned about having your kids in this business?'" Kevin Sr. told *Rolling Stone*. "But they're doing *Les Miz, La Bohème*—beautiful works of art." Kevin Sr. and Denise were proud of their boys, but they made sure they stayed grounded and focused on the important things in life, like family and helping others. Joe and Nick's theater careers were just taking off, but unfortunately for Broadway, neither Nick nor Joe would have time to commit to another show—they would be far too busy catering to a different type of audience.

CHAPTER 3
ALL TOGETHER NOW

With Nick and Joe performing on Broadway and all three boys going to auditions on a regular basis, things got pretty crazy for the Jonas household. Denise began homeschooling all three of the boys to make sure that their educations would stay on track despite all of the school they were missing. It also meant that the family had more time to spend together, which was good because it was about to get even bigger! On September 28, 2000, Frankie Nathanial Jonas was born. Nick, Joe, and Kevin were super-excited to have a new little brother. And Frankie has always wanted to be just like them, which means that someday Frankie might be rocking out onstage, too! As Frankie grew up, he earned the nickname

Frank the Tank, although fans sometimes refer to him as the Bonus Jonas. Frankie is the boss, according to his brothers, and he always gets his way. With his adorable smile and head of dark curls, Frankie will no doubt grow up to be just as good-looking as Kevin, Joe, and Nick.

Everything was going well and Nick had a lot to be thankful for, but he knew that there were many other kids who weren't so lucky. During the winter of 2002, Nick was performing in New York City almost every day. As he walked to and from the theater with his dad, he saw homeless kids and families in need of help. It broke Nicholas's heart to see so many children suffering when people were paying hundreds of dollars a night just to see him perform. He wanted to help them all.

So, with his family's help and the support of his church, Nick founded the Nicholas Jonas Change for the Children Foundation. The nonprofit organization was devoted to the needs of homeless, abused, and terminally ill children in the greater New York area. Nick really wanted to get other kids involved in helping their community. He rallied the support of his brothers, friends from church and school, and many of the other child actors on Broadway to help raise money and volunteer their time. When Nick's career really took off a few years later, he didn't have the time to personally drum up support, and without his tireless devotion, not as many people were donating money. The charity was put on hold for a while, but it has since been reborn as simply the Change for the Children Foundation and the Jonas Brothers donate 10 percent of their annual earnings to their charity!

In 2003, Nick got another chance to reach out and make a difference in his community. Nick and several other Broadway artists were asked to record classic Christmas songs for the annual Broadway Cares/Equity Fights AIDS CD, a compilation album to benefit AIDS research titled *Broadway's Greatest Gifts: Carols for a Cure, Vol. 4*. But none of the classic

Christmas songs seemed right when Nick was choosing what to sing. Nick wanted a song that really reflected how deeply concerned he was about the fate of the homeless and less fortunate during the Christmas season. So Nick and his father wrote "Joy to the World (A Christmas Prayer)." The lyrics were an emotional plea for peace and compassion during Christmas and all year long. With his song, Nick reached out to children who were starving, suffering, or alone, and he hoped that listeners would want to get involved in their own communities after hearing it. "Joy to the World (A Christmas Prayer)" tackled some very adult issues, but Nick knew that they were issues that needed to be addressed. Nicholas's dad recognized that they had created something truly special, so in November 2003, he sent a demo recording of Nick singing his song to INO Records, a Christian record label.

The executives at INO were blown away by Nick's emotional voice and mature stage presence.

They sent the song out to every Christian radio station across the country and it was quickly put into heavy rotation. Nick's song struck a chord with listeners, and within two weeks, it had the most increased airplay on the Hot Christian Adult Contemporary chart. "Joy to the World (A Christmas Prayer)" was, by far, one of the most popular Christmas songs that year. It was rereleased on October 3, 2006, on *Joy to the World: The Ultimate Christmas Collection*, a compilation of Christmas music from INO.

Nick must have been pretty proud of himself. After all, not everyone has a hit song on his first try! INO Records offered him a recording contract shortly after his song took off. INO had never signed such a young artist before, and they knew they were taking a big risk. According to Jeff Moseley, president of INO Records, "I entered into the idea of working with a twelve-year-old with fear and in trepidation. My fears have quickly resolved after realizing just how purposeful he is about what God has called him to do. He has an amazing sense of acuity when it comes to goals and dreams . . . In today's age with pre-manufactured pop, even as young as he is, Nicholas is a breath of fresh air as he has the ability to 'voice' his projects through his singing and songwriting." Kevin and Joe were very proud of Nick, and they were inspired by all of his success. The two older Jonas boys really began to take their music more seriously as Nick's career heated up.

With the help of his family, Nick worked on his album all through 2004, and that September, he was offered a very special opportunity. Nick was invited to sing "Joy to the World (A Christmas Prayer)" for the delegates at the United Nations to commemorate those who had lost their lives on September 11, 2001, when New York City's World Trade Center twin towers fell. The events of September 11, 2001, had had a huge impact on the Jonas family. Nick was especially heartbroken by the thought of the children who had lost parents in the fall. Nick felt very honored to be able to commemorate their deaths in front of such an influential audience, and he delivered a very moving performance.

Nick wrote the music for his INO self-titled debut album, *Nicholas Jonas*, with his dad and his brothers. Kevin and Joe helped Nick write eight out of the eleven songs for his CD. Not wanting to be left out, four-year-old brother Frankie tried to get in on the action, too. "He's doomed," Nick told *Clubhouse* with a laugh. "[H]e sat down at the piano and said, 'I'm writing a song.'" The boys drew inspiration from their own lives, and they wrote anytime and anywhere the inspiration struck. They even wrote one of the songs, "Time for Me to Fly," in the car on the way home from a Michael W. Smith concert!

Each of the boys brought something different to his songwriting, and the results were incredible. Serious Kevin was brilliant at finding the perfect lyrics when everyone else was stumped, and his creative guitar riffs gave the songs their catchy edge. Goofy

Joseph was great at adding in the fun, clever lyrics that would make the group popular later on, and Nick brought soulful vocals and ideas for inspirational tunes. Kevin Sr. helped his sons mix everything together to produce songs with a young, but polished, feel. Nick was thrilled to have the opportunity to share his music with the world. "This is my first record, so I'm very excited about this new experience and I am so blessed to have a family that is so loving and supportive of what I'm doing," Nick told About.com. "I hope this record touches a lot of people . . . The hope of this record is to make people feel good and happy inside. I'm excited to see what comes next."

In early 2005, Steve Greenberg, the incoming president of Columbia Records, heard a demo of Nick's album. "Only one thing really stuck out for me, which was this contemporary-Christian album by Nicholas Jonas," Steve told *Details*. "It wasn't a very good album. It was a very schmaltzy kind of record. But his voice was so good. I heard that voice and

I thought, *This is the best young person's voice that I've heard since Taylor Hanson. I've got to meet this guy.*" Steve invited Nick to give a showcase at Columbia.

Nick took the stage with Kevin and Joseph playing guitar and singing backup vocals. They played one of the songs they'd written together, "Please Be Mine." While watching the boys play together, something clicked for the folks at Columbia, especially when they heard that the boys had been considering performing together as a boy band like the Backstreet Boys or *NSYNC. "They were trying to write songs where they would stand onstage and dance—to be like a boy band," Steve told *Details*. "And I said, 'This is all wrong! You guys should . . . be a rock band!'" Steve had a very specific sound in mind for the boys, as he explained to Reuters.com. "I liked the idea of putting together this little garage-rock band and making a record that nodded to the Ramones and '70s punk."

Columbia asked Nick, Kevin, and Joseph if they would be interested in recording an album as a band,

and the boys accepted immediately. Nick told *Time for Kids* that he wasn't the least bit sad about losing out on a solo deal: "We are not competitive in our career. In our career we are very supportive of each other." Recording with his brothers would be three times as much fun!

They were on their way, but the brothers still had a lot of work to do. They needed to work in the studio with a new team of writers and producers to define their sound, write some songs, and, of course, come up with a name for their newly formed brother act. If anyone was up for the challenge, it was Kevin, Joe, and Nick!

CHAPTER 4

IT'S ABOUT TIME

Kevin, Nick, and Joe were well on their way to becoming the band their fans know and love today. But first, they had to record some songs. Columbia paired their new trio with some of the best songwriters and producers in the business to help the boys create some serious hits. Steve burned the boys CD after CD of punk songs from the seventies and eighties, hoping to inspire them to make a power-pop-punk album that would really catch the ears of teens. Steve Greenberg was the Jonas boys' biggest fan, and that meant a lot to the boys! Steve had a well-deserved reputation for taking young talents and turning them into big acts like Hanson, another famous brother act from the late 1990s. Kevin, Joe, and Nick had a lot of respect for Hanson and they hoped to appeal to the same fan base, so they listened closely to all of Steve's advice.

Some of the writers that they worked with included Adam Schlesinger (Fountains of Wayne), Michael Mangini (Joss Stone), Desmond Child (Aerosmith, Bon Jovi), Billy Mann (Jessica Simpson, Destiny's Child), and Steve Greenberg (Joss Stone, Hanson). Greenberg and Mangini are the Grammy Award-winning duo behind Joss Stone's two critically acclaimed albums. They produced the Jonases' first album. The boys were inspired by Steve's punk CDs, and they drew heavily on the upbeat sounds of the 1970s, British punk rock, and the grungy edge of garage rock. The result is "music on Red Bull," as Kevin puts it. "We actually wrote seven out of the eleven songs. We're really happy about the songs we got to write on the album, and we love the songs we didn't write," Joseph explained to YM.com. Kevin agreed. "We're absolutely blessed to have the songs that are on there. A bunch of other artists worked on our record, which is really cool; we got to work with some really great people. We're just really happy we got to make the record we wanted to."

The boys made demo recordings of over sixty songs for the album, and Joseph claims they wrote over a hundred. So what inspired them to write that many tunes? Nick explained it best to YM.com. "[W]e don't sit there and think about what people want to hear; we just write about something because we want to, like when we wrote the song 'Mandy,' we knew we needed an upbeat song for the record, but we didn't think about [what's going to be popular], we just wrote it, because it was important to us."

Each boy chooses subject matter for the songs differently. "For all of us, it's different things," Kevin told the *Montclair Times*. "Girlfriends, the family around us, people we've known . . ." But no matter who comes up with the ideas for the songs, the brothers all work together to write them. Kevin told

YM.com that sometimes they can hammer out a song in under an hour, but other times they will disagree and it can be stressful. "[W]e all work together, but that is something we fight about sometimes, not really anymore, but we went through that period about halfway through the album."

Joseph would often get upset that none of the songs seemed quite right, or Nick would feel that Joe and Kevin were ganging up on him, like he did when the boys were writing their hit song "Mandy." Nick came up with the lyrics for the line "and all those boy bands," and Joseph and Kevin thought the line was stupid. Luckily, Nick won that fight. "[N]ow it's the one line of the song the whole crowd sings," Nick bragged to YM.com.

The boys have a special method when it comes to writing music. Kevin explained the process to Scholastic.com: "We stand in a triangle and we will play with some chords on a guitar. Then, we will go over it with some melodies. Nicholas will try, Joseph will try, then I will try, and we continue growing. We got really good at it." If you ask the brothers who is the best at writing lyrics, they all answer the same way. "Kevin has this ability, like we'll just put something in his ear and it'll come out of his mouth," Nick told YM.com. "Like it'll process properly out of his mouth and comes out perfectly with a rhyme scheme and everything," Joseph added. But really, the boys all contribute pretty equally when it comes to writing their songs. Working with other writers was new for the boys—they'd never written with anyone besides one another and their father. The boys took all of the writers' advice to heart, and eventually they completed a number of songs they were very proud of.

It took over two years for the record company to be as satisfied—they kept pushing the album's release date back. Columbia really wanted to find a few more singles they thought could top the charts. Eventually, they asked the brothers to cover two songs by the British pop-punk band Busted. Busted is a little like the British version of the Jonas Brothers. The band is made up of three friends—Matt Jay, James Bourne, and Charlie Simpson. Busted has never become popular in America, so Columbia Records purchased the rights for two of their songs, "Year 3000" and "What I Go to School For." Kevin, Nick, and Joe had a great time recording the covers in the studio, and once the executives at Columbia heard them, they knew the album was finally ready.

The boys decided to call the album *It's About Time*, since so many of the songs were related to time, including "Time for Me to Fly," "Year 3000," "6 Minutes," and "7:05." The title of the album was especially appropriate since it had taken so long to get the album into stores and the Jonas Brothers were getting tired of waiting—for them it was about time that their journey to stardom really began!

CHAPTER 5

BUILDING THE BUZZ

While Kevin, Joseph, and Nick were patiently awaiting the release of their first album, Columbia Records sent them out to start a fan base the old-fashioned way—performing. The folks at Columbia didn't want to waste any time building buzz before the album dropped. The boys toured with some of the biggest names in music, including Kelly Clarkson, Jesse McCartney, the Backstreet Boys, and Click Five, through most of 2005. "We started touring this past summer. Our first show was with Jesse McCartney, and we had so much fun. That was in July. It started then and has been nonstop until now. We have a blast on the road playing every night. We've been to forty-five of the fifty states of America.

We're super-happy about that. My goal is to [tour] all of America in maybe two months," Nick told *Soundings* newspaper. While on tour they tried out different songs and different group names, trying to figure out exactly who they wanted to be as a band.

A band's name says a lot about them to their fans and potential fans, and Kevin, Joe, and Nick wanted to make sure they picked just the right name for themselves. But it took the band quite a while to hit on a name that everyone was happy with. They considered names like "Jonas 3," "Sons of Jonas," and the "Jonas Trio" before they finally settled on the Jonas Brothers by accident, as Nicholas explained to *Cross Rhythms*: "We thought of many different names for the band, and the label [was] thinking of Jonas 3 at the time, and we didn't like that at all. So during the first show we did, we got onstage and said, 'Hey! We're the Jonas Brothers.' That's just who we were, you know? And that was our name from then on because that's how people knew us."

The boys had often toured with their parents from church to church, but they'd never been on tour like that before. "[W]e were in a big red passenger van with a trailer hitched to the back with all our gear," Nick told *Rolling Stone*. "Big Bertha," Joe chimed in. "It had a dent in it, and we'd flip the seats around and call it . . ." "The Players Lounge," Nick finished, laughing. They were lucky if they managed to grab even six hours of sleep a night in that rickety van! It was a lot of hard work honing their stage skills while on the road. "[Most people] don't understand how much work it really takes," Nicholas told the *Kansas City Star*. "You have to keep doing it every day, trying . . . build up your voice throughout the entire day, and then you have a show at like ten o'clock at night." Joseph agreed. "It gets tiring, but, you know, the fact of when you get back on that stage, it's worth every bit. Every bit of energy that you spent to get there, it's completely worth it."

The Jonas Brothers played a new town almost

every day, and, as the opening act for major stars, they had to make sure their performances were high-energy, fun, and up to the same standards as the veteran performers'. "I'm pretty much stationary," Kevin told the *New Haven Register*, "just singing and playing my guitar. But Joseph and Nick, they run and do a ton. They jump around all over the place. Sometimes, if someone in the front row isn't paying attention, Joseph will run over and tap her on the shoulder and just start singing in her face. The time he did that, the girl just started freaking out and loving it. It's a way to get everyone involved."

With such amazing performers to learn from, Kevin, Joe, and Nick worked hard and perfected their stage show. But they weren't a huge hit at every show. They often played small venues alone in addition to opening for bigger bands, and they didn't always get the reaction they were hoping for. "We once played this show in Jersey," Nick told *Rolling Stone*. "It was, seriously, the most horrible little rock club in the world. It fit maybe 50 people. When we got there, the guy said there was a heavy-metal band the night before that blew out the PA system, so they'd have to take the monitors and spin them around." "It was out of control," added Kevin. "And our crowds were interesting." "*Curious*," Nick corrected him. "It had potential. Like it could be crazy. But it wasn't there yet." Thinking about those types of shows crack the brothers up now, but at the time it was easy to get a little discouraged. Eventually, though, real fans found the Jonas Brothers no matter where they were playing!

Soon the boys were gaining fans in every town thanks to their brotherly chemistry, insane energy, and, of course, supercute smiles. And as difficult as touring sometimes was, in the end, it was all worth it. "It really let us do a grassroots thing," Kevin explained to the *New Haven Register*. "We've gone to different places and played and started a buzz. The reaction back home on the East Coast has been overwhelming. Every show we play, we run back to the hotel and check our MySpace page and we've got a bunch of friend requests. It shows people are liking what they see."

Touring was getting better and better, but not everything was going as well. Nick was struggling on the road. He was constantly thirsty, cranky, and he had lost a lot of weight. Nick had always been cheerful and easygoing, so his bad attitude really worried his family. On a short tour break, Joe and Nick went off on a church retreat. That's when Joe finally realized how bad things were with Nick. "We went swimming, and he took his shirt off, and I freaked," Joe recalled to *Rolling Stone*. "He looked like a skeleton."

His family insisted on taking Nick to the hospital, where doctors diagnosed him with type one diabetes. Diabetes is an illness that affects how the body processes sugar. Basically, Nick's body doesn't produce enough of the hormone insulin to convert sugar into energy. At first, Nick was terrified that he was going to die and "I didn't know if we'd be able to continue as a band," Nick told *Rolling Stone*. But he bounced back quickly once the doctors explained what diabetes was and that he could live a fairly normal life. "After about the second day in the hospital, I realized that it'd be all right," Nick told *Rolling Stone*. "It would just take time and understanding to manage it."

Nick handles the disease bravely, as he told *Tiger Beat*. "Most of the kids who find that they have diabetes go immediately into shock and are devastated . . . I looked at it that way for about five minutes, and then I was like, 'This is an opportunity.' I knew that I wanted to make an impact somehow, and this is just another step I can take and I hope that kids can see the positive influence that they can have on other kids as a result of this, even if it's not diabetes. Even [if] it's a small illness that you have for a day—I mean, Kevin learned how to play guitar because he was home sick from school for a day, so he took that and made an opportunity from it. This is an opportunity for me to be a better person . . . [Y]ou have [to] pull yourself together and learn self-control and keep it cool. And I learn that every day."

Nick controls his diabetes with an insulin system called OmniPod, which gives him ten or more shots of insulin a day to keep his body processing food correctly. It is attached to his back and is wirelessly connected to a special gadget that Nick keeps in his pocket so he can monitor his blood-sugar levels at all times. But even so, Nick has to prick his finger up to twelve times a day to make sure his blood-sugar level is correct. It took almost nine months after being diagnosed before Nick felt like himself again. "Once you find a pattern with diabetes, you can have normalcy," he explained to *Rolling Stone*. Living with diabetes is not easy, but Nick has inspired kids with diabetes across the country not to let their illness hold them back from chasing their dreams.

With Nick's diabetes under control, the boys went back on the road. On top of practices, shows, writing new songs, and those oh-so-important six hours of sleep a night, the boys had schoolwork to do. All three brothers were homeschooled, and they started out every day on tour by getting their schoolwork finished, "because at night you're drained or in the middle of the day it's just like, you want to be able to focus and then that way you can do something fun. That's always good. We have hired tutors at home, but on the road, my work is like self-taught so I can teach it mostly to myself through the booklets," Nick told *Cross Rhythms*. Kevin and Joe have both graduated from high school since that first tour, but Nick is still working toward his diploma and he takes his studies seriously.

There were a lot of tour experiences that were really exciting for the Jonas boys. They loved getting to check out different towns and having the chance to hang out with other bands—especially bands that they really looked up to, like the Backstreet Boys. "It's crazy that one day I was singing Backstreet Boys songs in my basement—and just last week there I was onstage with them! Our dreams have really come true and we're so lucky," Nick said in a January 2006 press release from Columbia Records. It would have been easy to get caught up in the excitement of touring, but the boys always had family along for the ride to remind them of what was really important. "[W]e keep it a very tight-knit group. Our father's our comanager. Our road manager is our uncle. They're both pastors and they can both minister to us on the road. It's really a great thing to know that we have a tight and close group of people with us," Kevin explained to *Cross Rhythms*.

Toward the end of 2006, the Jonas Brothers signed on to do an Anti-Drug tour with Aly & AJ and the Cheetah Girls. Both of those groups packed some serious girl power and had some serious girl fans, which was just fine with the Jonas Brothers. They love having girl fans! The Anti-Drug tour went to schools across America to educate kids about the dangers of drug and alcohol use. This was a very important tour to Kevin, Joe, and Nick because they strongly believe that no one needs drugs or alcohol in their lives in order to be happy or have fun. They would never do drugs, and they wouldn't want any of their fans to use drugs, either. "We were totally for it, because we definitely want to make a difference," Joseph told the *Allentown Morning Call*. "We totally wanted to be a good influence." Most of the time, the bands would arrive at schools first thing in the morning. That meant the boys were up and ready by around 5 A.M. lots of mornings! The bands and managers would talk to the students about drugs and alcohol, and then the bands would perform. The performances were Joseph's favorite part, as he explained to the *Allentown Morning Call*: "It would be so funny because we would show up at the school, and it would be like seven o'clock in the morning. Kids would walk to school like, 'Oh, I want to go to bed'—totally super-tired, did not want to be in school that day. And we'd go, like, 'Okay, now here's the band,' and we would like totally rock out and the kids would go nuts."

The Jonas Brothers took a short break after a summer on the road and then opened for the Veronicas in early 2006. The Veronicas, a spunky twin sister act from Australia, were headlining their first tour to promote their album *The Secret Life of the Veronicas*, and the Jonas Brothers and October Fall were their two opening acts. "We're having a blast. We're going to schools every morning and playing shows with the Veronicas. Then we go to the venue for the night's show," Nick told *Soundings* newspaper. Touring with a sister act was extra fun for the three brothers, and they got along well with all of the other performers. The boys had started singing some of the songs they'd written for their upcoming album, and they loved introducing their fans to their new music. "We've known for a while how it felt to be onstage, but we never knew how it would feel to have people love music that we've written and which we both play and sing. It's very gratifying when fans come up to us after shows and tell us how much they relate to our songs," Joseph said in a January 2006 press release from Columbia Records. The boys were only on tour with the Veronicas for a few months, but it marked the end of almost a solid year of touring experience for the brothers. They had grown and matured a lot in that year and were more excited than ever to show the world just what they were capable of when their album was released.

CHAPTER 6

MOVING ON UP

The Jonas Brothers were certainly making headway with their touring, but they had yet to truly conquer the radio waves. "With our music we're trying to be successful. It's definitely a pop record. It's a pop/rock record for the mainstream . . . We just feel like this is where we belong—'this is who we are and let's just go for it!'" Kevin told *Cross Rhythms*. But with their album still awaiting a release date and with no released singles, it was difficult to get airtime. So the boys took matters into their own hands and posted recordings and silly videos on their MySpace page for their fans. And the fans definitely took notice. Every time Columbia announced a new release date for the album, the fans went nuts. Kevin, Joe, and

Nick appreciated the support. They were a little discouraged about their lack of a solid release date. After all, it had been almost a year since they had finished the album! But that holiday season, they got the best Christmas present they could have hoped for. Columbia decided to drop *It's About Time*'s first single, "Mandy," on December 27, 2005. The boys were absolutely thrilled with the news! "Mandy" was one of the songs Kevin, Joe, and Nick had written themselves and it was about one of their very close friends, so it was a very special song for all of them.

Once "Mandy" hit the radio waves, girls across the country were falling in love with Nick, Kevin, and Joe as they listened to the sweet and upbeat song they had written about their friend. But one girl was smiling every time she heard it, because she knew the song was actually about her. Mandy was a childhood friend of all of the Jonas boys, but she had been Nick's best friend when they were little. She and several of her friends were part of a sign-language group that had taken lessons from Denise Jonas. "Mandy and two other girls are part of this group called Signs of Love. They play music, write songs, communicate in sign language, dance, and everything. They went to nationals for it and they ended up winning second in the nation for the sign language group. My mom works with them. She loves sign language," Kevin told Scholastic.com. As Mandy, Kevin, Nick, and Joe got older, it was Joe who became close with her. They dated for a while and remain friends to this day. The boys actually wrote "Mandy" while Joe and Mandy were dating. How's that for romantic? Any girl would love to have such a sweet song written about her, and Mandy was no exception. Joe really put his heart into the lyrics. He sings about how silly and annoying he can be but how Mandy always understands him and cares about him no matter what happens.

And the boys didn't just write a song about Mandy—they also asked her to star in the three music videos for the song! How lucky can one girl get? The videos were directed by acclaimed music documentary filmmaker Ondi Timoner, and they really gave the boys the chance to show off their acting chops in a silly way. Timoner wanted to do something special for the Jonas Brothers' first music video, so she decided to shoot three videos to the same song! Each video would be for the song "Mandy," and each would tell one part of a longer story. The boys flew Mandy and her mom out to the set for their three-part video so that she could star as herself. But that's where the autobiographical part of the videos ends. Other than Mandy playing herself, the videos were purely fiction.

In the first video, Nick is watching Mandy in class. She drops her cell phone and he follows her, trying to return it. But when Nick catches up to her, Mandy's boyfriend, a popular jerk, starts bullying him. It cuts to Nick walking home alone. Suddenly, a large SUV starts chasing him. It ends with, "*To be continued . . .*"

The second video picks up with Nick being

chased by the large SUV. Inside are Mandy's boyfriend and his friends. Nick runs into the bushes and then hops into a car with Kevin and Joe. They pull into the street and drive off laughing at Mandy's boyfriend. Later that night at the prom, Mandy and her boyfriend are crowned prom king and queen. Mandy seems happy, but when it's time for her to go home, her boyfriend won't give her a ride. So the Jonas Brothers drive Mandy home, but when they get there, her father is furious at her for being late. He screams at her and hits her, and Mandy runs out of the house. She's about to jump back in the car with the Jonas Brothers when her boyfriend shows up and she can't decide which car to get into.

The third video picks up the next day with Mandy sitting in the backseat of her boyfriend's car as he and his friends drive around smashing mailboxes. She realizes that her boyfriend is a jerk and she's finally had enough! When they get to school, Mandy dumps him, and walks over to where Nick and Joe are hanging out. But Mandy's now ex-boyfriend isn't letting her get away that easily. He comes over and starts bullying Joe and Nick. Mandy runs across campus and gets Kevin. Kevin and Mandy hop into his car and drive over to Nick and Joe. Joe and Nick hop in the backseat, and they all drive away. The video ends with Mandy at the Jonas Brothers' concert, where the whole town (including Mandy's ex-boyfriend!) is there rockin' out to the Jonas Brothers' music. It was a pretty sweet ending.

The first of the three videos premiered on *TRL* on March 1, 2006. And the Jonas Brothers made their very first MTV appearance on the show to introduce their video. Kevin, Joseph, and Nick Jonas were incredibly excited. MTV is the biggest music channel on television and *TRL* was one of its most popular shows. In addition to watching their video's world premiere, the Jo Bros were also giving an interview with one of TV's hottest VJs, Vanessa Minnillo. The audience loved the video, and then the boys gave an interview where they really stole the show.

"This is Get to Know the Jonas Brothers," Vanessa announced. She quizzed the boys on their passions, musical influences, female fans, and rejection—and they answered every question like pros. But Nick really stood out.

"Nicholas, who do you think are the sexiest sisters: the Olsens, the Duffs, or the Hiltons?" Vanessa asked him.

"Um. Do you have a sister?" Nick answered sheepishly, flashing Vanessa a shy smile. His brothers whooped and gave Nick high fives as the girls in the audience let out a resounding, "Awwwwwww."

It was just a taste of how charming the brothers could be, but fans were hooked. They voted for the video like crazy, and the first "Mandy" video stayed on the *TRL* top ten for weeks, peaking at number four. The second video for "Mandy" also made it onto *TRL* for a few weeks. The third video premiered on *TRL*, but it never made it into the top ten. Seeing their music videos week after week on *TRL* must have been so exciting for Kevin, Joe, and Nick. Being featured on MTV is a huge step for any musician since MTV has the largest music fan base of any television channel in the country. With three videos for one song, the Jonas Brothers were getting a lot of exposure! "[T]he coolest feeling was when we debuted our video on *TRL*. We went to *TRL* and going up to that window and seeing four hundred screaming girls, fans, I mean!" Joe, laughing, told *Cross Rhythms*. "Seeing four hundred screaming fans, it's pretty awesome. It was awesome. It was a cool feeling."

Teenagers across the country were loving the Jonas Brothers—and so were several music supervisors who were choosing music for hot new movies and compilation CDs. On May 17, 2005, a track from Nick's canceled solo album called "Crazy Kind of Crush on You" was featured on the *Darcy's Wild Life* sound track. *Darcy's Wild Life* was a television series on Discovery Kids about a Hollywood actress and her daughter, Darcy (played by the beautiful Sara Paxton), who move from Los Angeles to the country. One of the other singles from *It's About Time* called "Time for Me to Fly" was featured on the sound track for the film *Aquamarine*. *Aquamarine*, also starring Sara Paxton, along with JoJo and Emma Roberts, is the story of two best friends who find a mermaid in their swimming pool and help her find love on dry land in return for one wish. And in March 2006, "Mandy" was featured on the Nickelodeon made-for-television movie special *Zoey 101: Spring Break-Up*. *Zoey 101: Spring Break-Up* is a movie special of the hit Nick series *Zoey 101* starring Jamie Lynn Spears. The producers liked "Mandy" so much that they also put it on the *Zoey 101: Music Mix* sound track album.

The boys were flattered that their singles were receiving so much attention, but what they really wanted was for fans to have the chance to hear their entire album. They finally got their wish on August 8, 2006, when *It's About Time* was released. But the results were a little discouraging. It was only a limited release of 50,000 copies and Columbia didn't do much in the way of advertising and marketing to help album sales. But even with a limited release, *It's About Time* reached number 91 on the Billboard 200 chart, which proved there were fans out there listening. Columbia might have been losing faith in the Jonas Brothers, but the fans weren't, and neither were Kevin, Joseph, and Nicholas. They knew they had what it takes to be major music stars, and they weren't going to let anything hold them back.

The Jonas Brothers worked hard and did everything they could to get fans excited about their first album. Shortly after the album was released, their second single, "Year 3000," dropped. It was popular with fans and was getting a decent amount of airtime on pop radio stations. But the song really became popular on Radio Disney. It was getting a tremendous amount of play, with tons of fans requesting more!

With all of that attention, Columbia decided

to premiere the music video for "Year 3000" on the Disney Channel instead of MTV. The boys shot a supercool video set in—when else?—the year 3000. They did most of the filming in front of a green screen. When the video was edited, the green screen was replaced with futuristic-looking buildings in a dome underwater! "We did some cool animation and graphic stuff, and all the girls have pink hair and [futuristic] outfits," Kevin told MTV.com. "It was fun to [shoot], 'cause when we got there, it was just really beautiful girls in futuristic costumes, and we were like, 'Ahhh,'" Joseph added.

Fans loved the "Year 3000" video, and album sales were holding steady, but Columbia just wasn't sure about the Jonas Brothers anymore. Steve Greenberg had left Columbia after a shake-up with management, and he had been the band's main supporter. The new management at Columbia wanted the boys to mimic other successful bands like blink-182, but Kevin, Nick, and Joe didn't want to be anyone but themselves. On top of all of that, Columbia wasn't supporting the band with advertising, marketing, and publicity the way that the boys had hoped they would.

So in February 2007, the Jonas Brothers parted ways with Columbia. It was a mutual decision—Columbia didn't feel that the Jonas Brothers could sell enough albums and the boys didn't feel that Columbia was providing them with enough opportunities. "The reason given to us was 'The indicators were not there,'" Kevin Sr. told *Rolling Stone*. "It was devastating." The Jonas Brothers had several successful tours and one fairly popular album under their belts, plus a huge fan base, but without a label they weren't going to get very far. They weren't ready to give up on their music, though, so they continued touring, although the family was struggling to keep the dream alive. "Our savings were spent, credit cards were maxed out," the boys' dad told People.com. "We were selling T-shirts for gasoline money at every gig." The brothers were shopping for a new label, but they didn't want to rush into anything. Luckily, their patience paid off, and it wasn't too long before they hit the label jackpot. The boys were moving to Hollywood.

CHAPTER 7

WELCOME TO HOLLYWOOD

Most bands would have called it quits after losing their label's backing, but not the Jonas Brothers. Bob Cavallo, the chairman of Buena Vista Music Group and a former manager of Prince, had been watching the Jonas Brothers for quite a while. So when Bob heard about their split from Columbia, he hurried to introduce Kevin, Joe, and Nick to Bob Iger, the head of Hollywood Records. Bob offered the boys a recording contract, and the boys jumped at the chance. Hollywood Records is the music arm of Disney, and it is the label of some of the hottest teen artists in the music business, like Aly & AJ, Hilary Duff, and the Cheetah Girls. "It was extraordinarily good fortune for us," Gary Marsh, the president of entertainment for Disney Channel Worldwide, told the *New York Times*. "We have so many other opportunities and extensions that we can use to launch and promote a group like this. And given who they are as people, their brand fits wonderfully with the Disney brand." Hollywood Records has a reputation for its nurturing, family-oriented vibe and its ability to launch teen artists to superstardom, and that was exactly what Kevin, Nick, and Joe were looking for. Hollywood Records and the rest of Disney were equally as excited to partner with the boys. "Kevin, Joe, and Nick are the real deal—incredible musicians, phenomenal performers, charismatic stars," Gary Marsh told E! Online. "An act like the Jonas Brothers doesn't come along very often. This is a giant coup for the Disney Channel."

Hollywood Records didn't waste any time putting their newest stars to work. The boys were excited to be collaborating with new producers and were eager to get back into the studio—but this time they were doing it their way. As beneficial as it had been for them to work with seasoned songwriters on their previous album, they really wanted their sophomore album to be their songs, their sound, and their chance to show their fans exactly what they had to offer. Luckily, Hollywood Records agreed. John Fields, who has worked with rock heavyweights like Rooney, Switchfoot, and Lifehouse, signed on to produce. Kevin, Joe, and Nick played him songs that they'd been working on since they had recorded their first album, and he loved them.

"When we signed to Hollywood," Kevin told starpulse.com, "we told the label, 'Hey, we have some demos of songs we've been writing for the past year and a half.' We thought it'd be so funny to just record those songs for the album to see what we could get away with. But those turned out to be the songs on the record!" Fields, along with Kevin Jonas Sr., worked with the boys to polish their songs and decide which singles to feature. Then the boys went into the studio and laid down eleven new tracks in just twenty-one days! In addition to writing and singing all of their songs on the album, they played the instruments for every song, too. Kevin played lead guitar, Joe played guitar and keyboards, and Nick played keyboards, guitar, and drums.

"The album was very much a collaborative process," Kevin told *SingerUniverse* magazine. "It's definitely our baby, but John completely understood our vision and made sure we were there to help him guide the process every day of the recording process. We rented out a house in Studio City that we called 'Rock House,' living there for the whole month of February and working from 11 A.M. to 11 P.M. in the attached facility called Underbelly Studios. It was a really awesome, one-of-a-kind experience."

They added two additional tracks to the album—"Kids of the Future," which they had recorded for the sound track of the Disney CGI film *Meet the Robinsons*, and "Year 3000," which was also on their first album. "Year 3000" was the most popular song with fans from *It's About Time*, and the brothers wanted to make sure that fans who hadn't been able to get their first album could have their favorite song. The boys decided to name the album *Jonas Brothers*. It was the first album that they had written entirely by themselves, and every song was personal—it was a true reflection of who they were, and they wanted their fans to know that immediately from the title. *Jonas Brothers* was released on August 7, 2007. It was the first album released with the new, Disney-created CDVU+ (CD View Plus) technology. When the CD is played on a computer, it gives fans access to a special digital magazine that contains exclusive pictures, desktop wallpaper, buddy icons, and other interactive goodies that can be accessed on- and off-line.

The boys celebrated the night of the release with a cruise around New York City. Kevin Sr. and Denise rented a yacht and invited all of Kevin, Joe, and Nick's friends and family to celebrate.

The brothers must have felt pretty blessed as they stood together on the deck of the boat, listening to their album and gazing out at the bright lights of Manhattan. Everything was finally falling into place—they had the perfect label and had just released a deeply personal album that they were truly proud of. What more could they ask for?

They may not have needed to ask for anything more, but they got it anyway! *Jonas Brothers* reached number five on the Billboard Hot 200 chart within a week of the album's release. Their first single, "Hold On," and its music video had been released two weekends before the album dropped and both were getting major airtime—on the radio and on the Disney Channel and MTV. The music video for "Hold On," which featured the boys playing in a very windy room, reached number two on *TRL*. "S.O.S." was released as the album's second single within a few weeks of the album's release, and fans loved it, too! The album has since sold over 1.4 million copies.

Hollywood Records was determined to put the Jonas Brothers on the map as the hottest new band in the business, and the boys appreciated all of their efforts. "There's definitely a huge top-forty plan in place for us by Hollywood Records with the new album," Kevin explained to *SingerUniverse* magazine. "[T]hey have been incredibly supportive of our music as it's evolved and of our desire to reach as many fans as possible. Through them, we've had the opportunity to work with some amazing video directors like Declan Whitebloom, but Disney has allowed us input into the creative direction of each one. On the first album, we got to write seven of the eleven songs, but on the new one, we wrote or cowrote all twelve tracks!" Nick added, "When we did *It's About Time*, it was the first record we had ever done, and we have so much more experience to draw from now, both from doing so many live shows to spending all that time in the studio. We've had two more years now to become more proficient on our instruments and do all the things we needed to become a better band. We were a much bigger part of everything that happened this time."

Like they did with their first album, the boys stuck to topics they knew when penning their catchy tunes for *Jonas Brothers*. They wrote songs like "Hello Beautiful," "When You Look Me in the Eyes," and "Inseparable" about falling in love, and songs like "S.O.S.," "Goodnight and Goodbye," and "Games" about the pitfalls of dating. They even threw in a few sad breakup songs, like "Still in Love with You," although it's hard to imagine anyone breaking up with one of the adorable Jonas boys! But perhaps the most telling song on the album is "Hollywood," which Kevin, Joe, and Nick wrote about leaving Columbia Records for Hollywood Records and their struggle to prove themselves all over again. The upbeat tune is a celebration of proving everyone wrong who doubted them. But Kevin, Joe, and Nick don't have any hard feelings against their old label. They believe that everything happens for a reason, and they knew that the move to Hollywood had been the best decision they'd ever made, and things were only getting better and better every day.

CHAPTER 8

ON THE ROAD AGAIN

With the boys' second album finished, Hollywood Records booked the brothers for public appearances and concerts, and set them up on the Jonas Brothers Summer 2007 Prom tour in June and July. The boys wanted to promote *Jonas Brothers* before it was released and reconnect with their fans, but they also had an ulterior motive: They wanted the chance to experience a prom! Since Kevin, Joe, and Nick had been homeschooled for most of high school, they never got to attend a high school dance or prom. The Prom tour was a huge success—after all, who wouldn't want to go to prom with the boys? The stage was set to look like a prom in a high-school gym, and there were several photo booths set up in the crowd so that fans could get prom pictures made. "The tour has been amazing. It is one of my favorite tours so far. We have visited states from California to New York. We even went to Puerto Rico," Nick told *Time for Kids*. The Jonas Brothers have just one request for fans at their concerts—don't throw hard things at the stage! "I had lip gloss thrown at my guitar, my *brand-new* guitar . . . I was so mad," Nick complained to YM.com—so stick to soft gifts like stuffed animals and flowers, girls! It must have been really cool for the boys to go back to high school (so to speak) for a few months, but don't worry, they have no plans to trade in their lives as a band for a regular high-school existence!

Their summer tour was especially sweet because it was sponsored by one of the brothers' favorite candies—Baby Bottle Pops! Kevin, Joe, and Nick inked an endorsement deal with Baby Bottle Pops in conjunction with Nickelodeon in early 2007. The band remixed the Baby Bottle Pop jingle and recorded it in fifteen-, thirty-, and ninety-second versions. Then they filmed a fun commercial to go along with the jingles—it was a blast! The boys rocked out for a crowd of extras and everyone had plenty of Baby Bottle Pops to snack on! "Our mom and our little brother, Frankie, came out too so the whole family was out for the video shoot. It was really cool. They actually got to be a part of it so that was nice and we also played a couple songs for the extras in the commercial so that was cool, too. It was just an awesome experience. It should be airing now," Kevin told teenmag.com. Nickelodeon and Baby Bottle Pops created a special website (www.bbpinvasion.com) where kids can access the Jonas Brothers' Baby Bottle Pops commercial, get special Jonas Brothers content like wallpaper and ringtones, and enter a sweepstakes to win a Jonas Brothers concert for their school. With Baby Bottle Pops sponsoring their tour, the brothers always had plenty of candy around, including extras of all of their favorite flavors. Joe loves strawberry, Nick can't get enough of watermelon and cotton candy, and Kevin's favorites are blue raspberry and watermelon.

The Jonas Brothers' second album, *Jonas Brothers*, was released as their Prom tour drew to a close. The boys were itching to get back on the road and perform their new songs for their fans. So when they were invited to be a part of the hottest tour of the year—Miley Cyrus's Best of Both Worlds tour—they immediately signed on.

CHAPTER 9
THERE'S SOMETHING ABOUT MILEY

Miley Cyrus is one of Disney and Hollywood Record's biggest stars, so getting the chance to tour with her was a dream come true for the Jonas Brothers. Miley has her own recording career, but she also plays Miley Stewart/Hannah Montana on the Disney Channel's hit series *Hannah Montana*. On the show, Cyrus's character Miley lives a double life. By day, she's Miley Stewart, a regular middle-school student, but at night she becomes Hannah Montana, pop superstar. In every episode, Miley struggles with her double identity and her desire to live a normal life despite her fame. Even though Hannah Montana is rich, famous, and adored by millions of fans, Miley Stewart is just a regular girl with regular problems, and fans of the show can definitely relate to that. With her pretty face, fabulous style, and powerhouse singing voice, Miley has inspired girls everywhere. Hollywood Records released a sound track for *Hannah Montana* featuring Miley singing as Hannah and the album reached number 1 on the Billboard Top Soundtracks chart. Hollywood Records knew they had the makings of a huge star on their hands, so they signed Miley to a record deal as herself, and she went straight into the studio to record another album, titled *Hannah Montana 2: Meet Miley Cyrus*. This album was different from any other album on the market—Miley would sing half of the songs as Hannah Montana and the other half as herself. Talk about life imitating art—Miley was suddenly living the same life as her character on TV; the only difference was that she didn't have to keep her multiple identities a secret! *Hannah Montana 2: Meet Miley Cyrus* was a huge success. It went platinum, selling over 2 million copies, and debuted at number 1 on the Billboard 200 chart.

Miley didn't just play a pop star on TV anymore—she really was one!

When Hollywood Records decided to send Miley on tour, they knew that her opening act would have to be pretty sensational to keep up with her. Luckily, they had the perfect band ready and waiting—the Jonas Brothers! The tour kicked off on October 18, 2007, and closed on January 9, 2008. They played fifty-four shows total, all of them completely sold out. It was *the* concert of the year. Tickets sold out in most places within a few hours of going on sale, and scalpers were reselling tickets online for hundreds of dollars! Kevin, Joe, and Nick were touring veterans by that point, but nothing could have prepared them for the overwhelming response from their fans on that tour. Getting to play for sold-out crowds of their dedicated fans was a dream come true for the brothers. Plus, the tour supported an amazing cause. One dollar for each ticket sold was donated to the City of Hope, a foundation that contributes to research for the prevention and cure of diseases that affect children around the world, like cancer. Giving back and rocking out? Nothing could be better than that as far as the Jonas Brothers were concerned.

They were also pretty psyched to be touring with Miley. The boys had become good friends with the singing starlet before the tour, so traveling with her was a lot of fun. "It will be our first arena tour. We are so excited to be able to have the opportunity to tour with one of our really good friends," Nick told *Time for Kids* before the tour began. The only person who wasn't thrilled about the boys touring with Miley? Frankie Jonas—the littlest Jonas has a big crush on Miley, and he was jealous that his brothers got to hang out with her so much. "I actually had a problem with my *little* brother, Frankie. You know Miley Cyrus from *Hannah Montana*, right? Well, I was saying that I thought she was cute and he was like, 'What!' and ran over and started trying to beat me up," Nick explained to YM.com. Joseph added, "He has a picture of her on his wall with a heart around her face." Uh-oh, Nick, you better watch out! But Frankie was right to be jealous. Nick and Miley did become very close, and ended up dating for two years. They kept their romance a secret, but after they broke up, Miley finally confirmed the rumors. "We became boyfriend and girlfriend the day we met. He was on a quest to meet me, and he was like, 'I think you're beautiful and I really like you.' And I was like, 'Oh, my gosh, I like *you* so much,'" Miley told *Seventeen*. Not many singers get the chance to tour with their girlfriend, so Nick was pretty lucky. And it's no wonder they fell in love so quickly since they were spending so much time together on tour. Miley really inspired Nick, and there are quite a few songs on the Jonas Brothers' third album that could be about her! The Disney power couple has since broken up, but they remain close friends and still care about each other deeply. It's just very difficult to keep a relationship going over long distances with such busy schedules!

Before the boys ever went on tour with Miley, they had the opportunity to get to know her when they filmed a guest spot on her show, *Hannah Montana*. The episode, titled "Me and Mr. Jonas and Mr. Jonas and Mr. Jonas," aired on August 17, 2007, right after the premiere of *High School Musical 2*, the made-for-television movie sequel to the smash hit *High School Musical*. Over 10.7 million viewers tuned in to catch the Jonas Brothers in their television series debut. In the episode, the boys play themselves, so it wasn't too much of a challenge to get into character!

On the show, the Jonas Brothers meet Miley Stewart in her Hannah Montana disguise at a recording studio and hit it off—but not with Miley/Hannah. Instead the boys bond with Miley's dad, Robbie Ray (who is played by Miley's real-life dad, Billy Ray Cyrus). Robbie Ray writes all of Hannah's songs, and he agrees to write a song for the Jonas

Brothers. As the boys bond with Robbie Ray through prank phone calls, silly games, and lots of horseplay, Miley becomes jealous. She tries to regain her father's attention, but when nothing she does seems to work, she decides to take matters into her own hands. Miley and Lily dress up as two boys and convince the Jonas Brothers that they wrote the song Robbie Ray has been working on. In a hilarious scene set in a recording studio, Miley and Lily, dressed as two very strange-looking boys, have a showdown with the Jonas Brothers. Their plan almost works, but Robbie Ray arrives and sets things straight. He and Miley have a heart-to-heart and Robbie Ray decides the song would be best as a duet with Hannah Montana and the Jonas Brothers. At the end of the episode, Hannah and the Jonas Brothers perform the song "We Got the Party," which became an instant hit on the Disney Channel. "[I]t's just a fun song; we love it. Actually some of the funniest parts of the show were when we were hanging out with the cast," Nick told Tommy2.net.

Filming with the cast and crew of *Hannah Montana* was a great experience for the Jonas Brothers. They had a blast joking around with Miley and Emily and playing with the fun props from the episodes—including toy guns that shot foam balls. The boys helped Miley when she forgot lines during rehearsals, and Kevin coached Emily on "being a dude" when she was getting ready for her scene dressed up like a boy. During breaks in rehearsals and shooting, the boys would entertain the crew by singing their favorite songs from the 1980s and dancing around. It was especially fun for Nick, since he got plenty of flirting time in with Miley on set! All of that goofiness and energy from rehearsals definitely helped when it was time to film—Kevin, Joe, and Nick gave an amazing performance that proved they had real talent as actors.

CHAPTER 10

MEETING THE MOUSE

Even before the Jonas Brothers signed on with Hollywood Records, the big shots at Disney were impressed with the Jonas Brothers' talent and invited them to record some very special songs. For *DisneyMania 4*, the brothers did a cover of "Yo Ho (A Pirate's Life for Me)," a song made famous in the Pirates of the Caribbean ride at the Disney theme parks. The *DisneyMania* compilation albums always feature the hottest new stars performing their own versions of classic Disney songs. The Jonas boys must have been thrilled to record "Yo Ho." All three of them love to ham it up when acting a part, so performing as pirates gave them plenty of opportunities to get into character. The finished recording was one of the highlights of the album. Disney was so impressed with the Jonas Brothers' energy, professionalism, and sound that Disney asked them to record a new version of the theme song for their animated series *American Dragon: Jake Long*.

American Dragon is a cartoon about a Chinese-American boy named Jake living in New York City who discovers that he, along with everyone else on his mother's side of the family, can transform himself into a dragon. The cartoon's action-packed storylines and hilarious characters have made it a favorite with Disney Channel viewers. The Jonas Brothers' version of the theme song replaced the original version in the summer of 2006. The boys must have been really excited to hear their song kicking off such a popular show!

The Jonas Brothers became fast fan favorites on Radio Disney after the release of their single "Year 3000," so when Disney was planning a special tenth-anniversary celebration for their radio station, they just had to have the Jonas Brothers there. The boys performed along with other hot groups like Aly & AJ, Miley Cyrus, the Cheetah Girls, and Bowling for Soup. "I think one of my favorite concert[s] so far has been the Radio Disney 10th Birthday show—that was an amazing night," Nick told Musicxcore.com. "It's kind of like, 'Oh, let's play the best venue ever' kind of night," Kevin added. Radio Disney's Totally 10th Birthday Concert was held on July 22, 2006, at the Arrowhead Pond in Anaheim, California, and was broadcast live on Radio Disney.

After that thrilling concert, Kevin, Joe, and Nick were excited to pair up with Disney again to record a cover of "Poor Unfortunate Souls" from the classic Disney animated feature *The Little Mermaid*. "Poor Unfortunate Souls" is the signature song of Ursula, the sea witch, in the original movie. She sings it to Ariel when convincing her to give up her voice for a pair of human legs. Originally it was a slinky, evil ballad, but the Jonas Brothers definitely put their own spin on it. They sped up the tempo and infused the lyrics with a gravelly feel. The boys also filmed a music video for the song. They kept a water theme by filming at a community swimming pool where there were so many rules it was impossible to have fun. The Jonas Brothers show up and lead the kids hanging out at the pool in a mini-rebellion. Kevin, Joe, and Nick encourage the kids at the pool to break all of the rules, including jumping into the pool during adult swim! The video ends with everyone swimming and having a blast. Both the video and the Jonas Brothers' recording of "Poor Unfortunate Souls" were included on a two-disc special edition release of *The Little Mermaid* sound track in October 2006.

Once the Jonas Brothers officially signed on with Hollywood Records in early 2007, they were put right to work. The first thing that Hollywood asked of their newest stars was to record a few more songs for sound tracks and compilation albums while they were waiting for the release of their sophomore album. So the boys went into the studio and pumped out several catchy, high-energy songs. On March 27, 2007, two albums were released simultaneously featuring the Jonas Brothers: *DisneyMania 5* and the *Meet the Robinsons* sound track. The boys recorded a cover of "I Wanna Be Like You" from the Disney animated film *The Jungle Book* for *DisneyMania 5*. They gave the song a seriously punk-rock edge and recorded a fun video for the song with a jungle theme. The video and song are featured on *The Jungle Book* Platinum Edition DVD, which was released in September 2007. In an interview on Disney's *Super Short Report*, the brothers were asked which *Jungle Book* character they are most like. Nick thinks he's most like King Louis, because, as he put it, "I'm the king." Joseph identifies most with Baloo the bear because he thinks he gives the best bear hugs.

After monkeying around recording "I Wanna Be Like You," Kevin, Joseph, and Nicholas recorded a song for the sound track of *Meet the Robinsons*, a Disney CGI animated feature film about an orphan boy named Lewis who travels to the future. The Jonas Brothers recorded a song called "Kids of the Future" for the sound track. It was a rewrite of Kim Wilde's "Kids in America." "Kids of the Future" is a positive, punk affirmation of the film's themes of love, acceptance, and family. The boys also filmed an amazingly cool video to go along with the song. The video scenes from *Meet the Robinsons* are intercut with the Jonas Brothers rocking out on a futuristic set. The video premiered on the Disney Channel and was played often, thanks in part to fan requests.

On August 25, 2007, the Jonas Brothers got their first real taste of life as Hollywood Record performers. They were the main attraction as they rocked out for a screaming crowd at the closing ceremonies of the Disney Channel Games in Orlando, Florida. The Disney Channel Games are a series of competitions that Disney puts on every summer. Stars from Disney Channel series and made-for-television movies are divided into teams and compete against one another in fun events, like obstacle courses, Extreme Rock Paper Scissors, and Super Soccer. The games take place over the course of the summer and are watched by millions of viewers, so the closing ceremonies are a big event. It was a fun concert for the boys, especially since many of their good friends were competing in the games!

The Disney Channel Games closing ceremonies concert was so popular with fans that the Disney Channel decided to have the Jonas Brothers headline a special televised concert in October 2007 called *The Jonas Brothers in Concert*. The brothers performed songs from *Jonas Brothers* and *It's About Time* for fans in New York City's Gramercy Park. The boys loved having the chance to rock out in New York, especially since they grew up seeing concerts there!

Then, for the 2007 holiday season, the Jonas Brothers contributed a song called "Girl of My Dreams" to *A Disney Channel Holiday*, a compilation album of holiday songs by hip young bands and musical artists. The album also includes tunes by Corbin Bleu, Miley Cyrus, Ashley Tisdale, the Cheetah Girls, Billy Ray Cyrus, and Keke Palmer. The brothers appeared in the 2007 Walt Disney World Christmas Day Parade. It would have been nice for the boys to be home for the holidays in New Jersey, but it was even cooler for the whole Jonas clan to spend Christmas at Disney World! They got to go on tons of rides, hang out at the beach, and be a part of one of the coolest parades anywhere. After all, not everyone gets to be in a parade with Mickey Mouse, Donald Duck, Goofy, and the rest of the Disney gang!

Then, in 2008 the brothers signed on to compete in the Disney Channel Games for the first time. They surprised fans by splitting up to participate on different teams. "We really enjoyed the competition against one another," the Jonas Brothers told Scholastic.com. "It was intense!" The events included things like Extreme Rock Paper Scissors and Hamster Ball Bowling. It was an especially exciting time to compete, since the Disney Games took place at the same time as the 2008 Olympic Games in Beijing. "The Disney Channel Games are more fun," Jennifer Stone of *Wizards of Waverly Place* told Scholastic.com. "The Olympics are more serious because they have been training for them their entire lives." All of the Disney stars were pretty fun to watch during the games, and the games gave the Jonas Brothers the chance to get to know some of the other Disney stars better. It was definitely a cool way to spend part of their summer!

But before Kevin, Joe, and Nick battled it out in the D.C. games, they had to battle it out with another Disney star on the small screen—Miss Piggy from the Muppets! The boys were invited to be a part of the first of many Disney Channel *Studio DC: Almost Live* specials. The show paired Disney stars with everyone's favorite Muppets for skits, performances, and dances. Kermit the Frog, Miss Piggy, Animal, Gonzo the Great, and the Swedish Chef were some of the big Muppet performers on the show. For the Jonas Brothers' segment, Miss Piggy claimed to be their long-lost sister, Joan S. Jonas, and performed a hilarious version of "That's Just the Way We Roll" with the boys. Working with a Muppet was a little challenging, since ignoring the puppeteer giving life to Miss Piggy wasn't easy to do while singing, but it was amazingly cool for the brothers to perform with such a skilled entertainer. After all, the Muppets have been around since the 1970s! And once they got used to having the puppeteer around, it was easy to interact with Miss Piggy. The show aired on August 3, 2008, and was a big hit with Disney viewers.

The Jonas Brothers loved everything they were doing with Hollywood Records and Disney, but they still had another area of entertainment that they wanted to break into more seriously—acting.

CHAPTER 11

THEY ROCK!

Making their guest appearance on *Hannah Montana* gave the Jonas Brothers their first taste of acting for television. The brothers had already worked on Broadway and in commercials, but acting for TV was different. The brothers gave such incredible performances that when the folks at the Disney Channel began work on their next original made-for-television movie, they made sure to include roles for the Jonas Brothers. So Kevin, Nick, and Joe headed off to summer camp, Jonas style. The movie was called *Camp Rock* and they filmed it at Camp Wanakita in Haliburton, Ontario, and Kilcoo Camp in Minden, Ontario, Canada.

In the film, Kevin, Joe, and Nick star as the

members of a band named Connect 3, who came together while attending Camp Rock, a special summer camp for aspiring musicians. Kevin played Jason, Nick played Nate, and Joe played the bad boy of the group, Shane Gray. "We grew up at this camp called Camp Rock. You know, that's where we learned to play, that's where we learned our sound, you know, that's where we became a band. And when Shane Gray gets a really big head on his shoulders and starts becoming this ultimate diva—in a sense or divo—we can't take it anymore. We end up sending him back to Camp Rock to be a counselor and find himself. And we end up canceling our tour. So he goes back to Camp Rock and kind of starts the process of getting back to who he was—not caring about the image, not caring about what people think of him, more about the music and what the real meaning is. And it's amazing. There are a lot of really funny jokes in it about record labels and stuff like that," Kevin told Scholastic.com. "We're really excited because it's a film that my brothers and [I] got to be a part of, you know. I play Jason. My brother Nick plays Nate and then Joe, Shane Gray. Shane Gray is . . . I'll say the lead singer, [but] not really. It's like we are pretty much the same entity as the group that we do in real life. But he kind of gets a really big head on his shoulders," Kevin explained to Scholastic.com. Shane Gray is a major celebrity in the film. All of the girls at Camp Rock go nuts when they discover that Shane is one of their counselors. Having him there inspires all of the campers to perform even better than they would have normally, but it also ups the competitive vibe at camp. Every girl wants to catch Shane's attention, so the pressure is really on to shine.

At camp, Shane meets a young girl named Mitchie with a big voice and even bigger dreams. Shane hears Mitchie singing, but doesn't see her, on one of the first days of camp and spends the rest of the summer trying to find the girl behind the song. Mitchie's mom works as the camp cook so she can afford to send Mitchie to camp, and Mitchie helps out between her classes. Mitchie is embarrassed about her family's lack of money and lies about it to impress the popular kids, but it's difficult to live a double life. Demi Lovato, the Disney newcomer who plays Mitchie, told Scholastic.com, "Mitchie is pretty shy. She was insecure at first, but she realizes who she is at the camp and comes into her own. I can relate to her because I was the same way before I started the movie. When I was filming in Canada, I really found out who I was . . . As I was doing the scene where I rock out on stage at the end, I evolved. It was really cool. But I don't like liars, and she tends to lie to have a good reputation, but it's innocent. Her intentions aren't mean, but she just gets caught up in the crowd there. I don't like that!" Eventually, Tess, the meanest girl at camp, played by Meaghan Martin, figures out the truth and exposes Mitchie in front of everyone. For a while Mitchie is the camp outcast, but eventually she finds her own voice with the help of her new friend

Caitlyn. The one bright spot for Mitchie is that she and Shane have started a flirtatious friendship, but that only makes things more difficult with Tess and her friends. Shane has no idea that Mitchie is the girl he's looking for until the final show at camp. There, Mitchie stuns everyone by singing one of her original songs and then Shane joins her onstage for a final number and a kiss!

The Jonas Brothers knew as soon as they read the script that it was the perfect project for them. Not only did they get to act, but they also got to perform a few musical numbers, which they knew their fans would appreciate. Plus they got to work with a cast full of powerhouse Disney stars like Alyson Stoner, Meaghan Martin, and newcomer Demi Lovato. The boys gave the film their all. They even got so into their characters that they began improvising and adding their own touches to the script. "Music and acting are definitely, definitely different. We've been so blessed to be able to use both of them at the same time. Even in *Camp Rock* we got to act but also add in so much of our own stuff," Kevin told Scholastic.com. Some of the funniest moments in the movie are ones that the Jonas boys made up on the spot. Kevin, in particular, really hammed it up in front of the cameras. Fans of the Jonas Brothers YouTube videos already knew how funny they could be, but their comedic skills were a pleasant surprise to a lot of people. They got such a great response to their performances that it really got the boys thinking about future projects. "Acting is really cool. You know, as a band we, we love to act as well as sing, and I think it'd be a major part in our career as well. And we hope to be the kind of artists [who] can sing, perform, go on tour and act as well," Nick told Scholastic.com.

All of the brothers rocked in the movie, but it was Joe who really had the starring role this time. "It seemed like out of the three of the brothers, he was the right guy for that role," Gary Marsh told the *New York Times*. Joe loved the challenge of portraying a character that really grew and changed over the course of the film, plus he could really relate to Shane. "We have a lot of similarities. For one, Shane tours a lot and I can see how easy it is for things to get to your head. I'm not like him because I have great parents and they keep us grounded. We don't take advantage of everything we get. I think Shane definitely did. It's fun playing his character because you're allowed to be mean," Joe told *Teen* magazine.

One of the biggest perks of playing Shane was acting opposite Demi Lovato, the gorgeous newcomer who played Mitchie. Demi was super-nervous to act opposite one of the cutest guys in music, but she got over that pretty quickly. "The first *Camp Rock* scene I filmed was with Joe, so you can just imagine—any 15-year-old would be nervous! In the scene, I threw flour on my face, and filming took 30 minutes, so I had this white, filthy powder all over my face! This was one of our first conversations, and I was just totally embarrassed," Demi told Scholastic.com. Luckily, Joe put her at ease, joking with her and being his goofy self. Demi became close friends with all three Jonas boys. She's into music as well, and the three would have great jam sessions in between takes! Demi can't say enough nice things about the Jonas boys. As she told Scholastic.com, "Joe is a big dork [laughs]. Nick is witty and sarcastic—sometimes I think he is the funniest. Kevin plays the older-brother role. They're all really, really great."

Kevin, Joe, and Nick got along well with all of their costars. The entire cast would get together in the evenings to hang out. They would order pizzas, put on music, talk, or, everyone's favorite, have dance parties! "[W]e used to have a lot of dance parties in the hotel room, and one night, we were just dancing and Nick all of a sudden made up this new dance move. It's like his signature dance move now, and he does it all the time! And it's just hilarious because we were just kind of messing around, and he did this move with his arms, and we're like, 'That's awesome! You should do that all the time!' And now he does," Meaghan Martin told Scholastic.com. "It's like an elbow, arm move. He puts his elbows . . . it's like one arm at a time, and he puts them down, and then he sticks them out, and he spreads his hands out and then claps, if that makes any sense at all—which it probably doesn't!" With all of the off-camera singing, jamming, and dancing it was probably a lot like going away to a performance summer camp for the stars.

All of that off-camera creativity really paid off in an unexpected way. Demi had just signed with Hollywood Records and was gearing up to record her debut album when they were filming *Camp Rock.* So Kevin, Joe, and Nick helped her write some songs. The folks at Hollywood were so impressed with the collaboration that they asked the Jonas Brothers to help produce Demi's album, and set up Demi to open for the boys' 2008 Burnin' Up summer tour. The guys were thrilled. Demi was a blast to hang out with and the boys were very impressed with her musical skills.

They knew she would fit right in on their tour. Of course, with Demi playing Joe's love interest in *Camp Rock*, touring with them, and having them produce her album, she was spending a lot of time with the brothers. Rumors began to swirl that she was dating Joe. But Demi is just close friends with the boys, and is not romantically involved with any of them!

Leaving behind all of their new friends once filming wrapped was hard for the boys. Luckily, they did get a chance to reunite to record the *Camp Rock* sound track and for the film's premieres. And the *Camp Rock* premieres were big ones! The party and screening the stars attended in Los Angeles and London were fun, but the stars were stunned when they heard just how many viewers across the country had tuned in to see the movie. In its first showing on the Disney Channel, it garnered 8.9 million viewers. On its second showing the next night on ABC, 3.6 million tuned in. And on its third showing on Disney Family, 3.7 million fans watched. The sound track was also a smash-success. It debuted on June 17, 2008, at number 3 on the Billboard Hot 200 chart, sold more than 188,000 copies in the first week alone, and has sold almost 1 million copies to date.

Of course, the Jonas Brothers were psyched that their first big Disney acting project had been so successful! And Disney was so pleased with *Camp Rock* that they signed Joe, Kevin, Nick, Demi, Alyson, Meaghan, and the rest of the cast up for a sequel. *Camp Rock 2* will debut in summer 2009, and while a script hasn't been nailed down yet, the rumor is that it might feature the *Camp Rock* kids battling it out with a rival camp! And this time, Kevin and Nick are likely to have bigger roles. It will have more great music, plenty of drama, and a little extra romance. So stay tuned to see what the sequel has in store for all of your favorite *Camp Rock* characters!

CHAPTER 12

J*O*N*A*S

With the success of *Camp Rock* and their hilarious guest shot on *Hannah Montana*, Disney couldn't deny the Jonas Brothers' star power. So the next logical step for the band was to expand their television horizons. The folks at Disney had some seriously cool ideas for their stars, including a behind-the-scenes mini documentary series to debut in spring 2008 and a half-hour comedy series for fall 2009.

The Jonas Brothers loved both ideas, especially the thought of giving fans a look at just what goes on in their lives when they aren't performing. The series, titled *Jonas Brothers: Living the Dream*, was made up of five ten-minute segments that aired between shows on the Disney Channel. The segments showed fans everything that went on while the Jonas Brothers were on tour. Fans got to see the boys designing their stage for their next tour, working on new songs, choosing their wardrobe, hanging out with their family and friends, and playing goofy pranks, as well as, of course, footage of the brothers' performances. The segments quickly became a favorite of Disney viewers. Seeing just how normal and grounded the adorable brothers are only made fans love them even more.

Next, Disney presented Kevin, Joe, and Nick with the concept for a television series called *J.O.N.A.S.* In the pilot, Kevin, Joe, and Nick star as three brothers in a band called the Jonas Brothers who tour the country in a rickety tour bus with their father—this part wasn't much of a stretch for the boys! But the band is just a cover—the boys and their dad are really spies. In addition to being their last name, *J.O.N.A.S.* stands for Junior Operatives Networking as Spies. They spend a lot of time trying to keep their spy jobs a secret from their mother, friends, and the media, especially a teenage reporter named Stella Malone who wants an inside look at the band. Their arch nemesis is Dr. Harvey Fleischman, an evil dentist whose ultimate goal is to gain control over teenagers everywhere. "We went through a week and a half of martial arts training to get ready for it," reports Kevin to the *National Ledger*. "We had to do stunts. We were on cables and all that kind of stuff, and it was absolutely awesome. We actually trained with a guy named Koichi [Sakamoto]; he's the man who trained the Power Rangers, which was exciting for us." The guys were really pleased with the finished pilot and kept their fingers crossed that Disney executives would like it—and they did! In October 2007, Disney announced that they were adding *J.O.N.A.S.* as one of their new series for 2008. But then there was a change of plans. Kevin, Joe, and Nick had just finished their tour as the opening act for Miley Cyrus on her Best of Both Worlds tour when they got the news that Disney wanted to rework the show.

The spy stuff was exciting, but it wasn't very realistic. Fans had had such a positive response to *Living the Dream* that the Jonas Brothers and Disney wanted to build on that idea. Kevin, Joe, and Nick are big fans of HBO's *Flight of the Conchords*, a show all about a band struggling to make it big. It's shot in a gritty documentary style and is incredibly funny. They decided to make their show more like that. The title was switched slightly to become *J*O*N*A*S*, and it's all about the Jonas Brothers living their everyday lives in the spotlight. "We can just pick up a guitar and break into song—in really funny situations," the boys told Ryan Seacrest on his KIIS-FM morning show. All of the episodes are fictional, but some of the funnier moments are loosely based on things that have happened to the boys! "It's going to be about us as a band but dealing with normal things, like trying to take out the trash and how not to get hounded by fans," Joe told *ELLEgirl* magazine. "It's going to be a funny show, and it's going to be a great cast." All three of the brothers have been very involved with every aspect of the show creatively. "It is going to be really cool. We are helping to design the show, from the clothing to the set design," Joe told Usmagazine.com. With the Jonas boys being so vocal about the creative direction of the show, there is a good chance that they will bring in some of their close friends as guest stars!

The best part of filming the show was that the boys got to stay in L.A. for five months. They hadn't spent that long in one place in what seemed like forever, so even though they worked long hours on their television set, it was still nice not to be on the road! They got to spend a lot of time with their family and all of their friends who are based in Los Angeles, like fellow Disney stars Selena Gomez, Demi Lovato, Emily Osment, Mitchel Musso, and Miley Cyrus. They are definitely looking forward to shooting season two just to have another break like that!

The show is set to premiere in May or June 2009, so be on the lookout for this sure-to-be-hilarious show on the Disney Channel!

CHAPTER 13

LIVE LIKE NEVER BEFORE

With all of the success the Jonas Brothers were having with their second album and their acting endeavors, fans were more eager than ever to see the boys perform live. They had toured with some of the biggest names in music, but what the Jonas Brothers were really interested in was headlining their own arena tour so that they could reach out directly to their fans. In early January 2008, they got their wish. The boys signed a two-year promotion deal with Live Nation. Live Nation is known for its big-name clients like Madonna, U2, Jay-Z, Nickelback, and Shakira. The Jonas Brothers were the youngest act ever to be signed by the prestigious concert promotion company, and it definitely made the rest of the music industry stand up and take notice of just exactly what the Jonas Brothers were accomplishing.

The boys kicked off their first concert tour with Live Nation on January 30, 2008. It was called the Look Me in the Eyes tour and it lasted for two months. At every show, they performed songs from *Jonas Brothers*, plus a few songs from their third album *A Little Bit Longer*, which wouldn't be released for months. Fans were psyched to get a sneak peek of the Jonas Brothers' newest songs, and the show sold out in almost every city. It was a huge success for their first headlining tour, but what really made the Look Me in the Eyes tour different for Kevin, Joe, and Nick was the fact that the entire tour was captured on film. A Disney camera crew chronicled all of the ups and downs of touring for the Disney reality series *Jonas Brothers: Living the Dream*. The footage was edited into short segments that began airing on the Disney Channel on May 16, 2008. Having a camera crew around made the tour buses even more crowded, but it was also a blast. All of the Jonas boys love hamming it up for the camera, as the cameramen quickly learned!

Next, the boys joined Canadian bad girl Avril Lavigne for a month of her Best Damn Thing tour in Europe. The Jonas Brothers opened for Avril along with Boys Like Girls. Kevin, Joe, and Nick all love Avril for her tough, in-your-face attitude and her punk style. They are also big fans of Boys Like Girls' catchy, fast-paced tunes. Kevin, Joe, and Nick's album, *Jonas Brothers*, had just been released in Europe in June, so it was the perfect opportunity for them to promote the album to their European fans. The tour schedule was incredibly hectic, but the boys hadn't really gotten much of a chance to go overseas, so it was a treat for them, even if they didn't get to do much sightseeing while they were there!

A month after returning from Europe, the Jonas Brothers kicked off their Burnin' Up tour on July 4, 2008. They were promoting their soon-to-be released third album, *A Little Bit Longer*, and the sound track for their Disney Channel movie *Camp Rock*, but they also performed favorites from *Jonas Brothers* and *It's About Time*. It was the biggest tour the boys had ever done. Twelve tour buses and twelve trucks carried more than one hundred crew members, including the Jonas family, the backup band, caterers, roadies, and security (plus all of the boys' equipment) from venue to venue. The crew included some of the best in the business, including Big Rob, the boys' bodyguard, Felicia Culotta, their personal assistant, and manager Johnny Wright, all of whom used to work for Britney Spears. In fact, nine members of the boys' crew worked for Britney at some point! But the Jonas fans definitely beat the Britney fans in devotion and excitement. "There are times when it gets crazy," Nick told People.com. "Girls jumping, police holding them back. It's amazing." The boys have even dedicated one of their tour buses for fans to sign at concerts! By the end of the tour, that bus was covered in so many messages, names, and phone numbers that it was almost impossible to read. And it wasn't just teen girls getting excited; parents love them, too! Kevin, Joe, and Nick always perform a few covers for the parents in the audience, like Shania Twain's "I'm Gonna Getcha Good." "It's fun to see the parents when that song comes on, especially the moms," Kevin told E! Online. "They're like, 'Oh my God! Wow! They're really playing our favorite song.'" It was *the* concert of the summer and tickets sold out within a day at almost every venue! The tour opened in Ontario, Canada, but the boys returned to America shortly after for two very special performances.

With all of the touring Kevin, Joe, and Nick had been doing, a lot of their fans had gotten the opportunity to see them perform live. But even the Jonas Brothers haven't made it to every town in America. So when Hollywood Records and Disney proposed the boys film a 3-D concert special, the Jonas Brothers jumped at the chance. The Miley

Cyrus/Hannah Montana Best of Both Worlds 3-D concert had been a huge hit with fans, and the Jonas Brothers loved the idea of giving their fans the same experience.

Kevin, Joe, and Nick had seen Miley's 3-D film and, while hers was awesome, they wanted theirs to be even bigger and better! They followed the same format she had used, with behind-the-scenes documentary-style segments combined with concert footage from two performances from their Burnin' Up tour. "We can't wait to start working on this film for our fans," Kevin, Joe, and Nick said in a press release before filming began. "It's going to be awesome and we really want to bring a totally unique and different movie experience to everyone whether they've seen us live or not." To achieve that, the boys kept the 3-D element of the film in mind when designing the tour. They wanted to make sure there were lots of elements, like lasers, lights, smoke, and other cool stuff that would really pop in 3-D! On July 13 and 14, a

Disney Digital 3-D production crew filmed the boys in Anaheim, California performing songs from all three of their albums to use for the film. The Jonas Brothers always put on an incredible show, but they worked hard to give the best performances of their lives when the cameras were rolling. They wanted to really connect with fans, and it totally worked! The film is phenomenal, and in 3-D it really seems like the boys are singing just to you when you watch it.

To really make the movie sensational, the boys wanted to have a guest star performer. So Kevin, Joe, and Nick asked teen country crooner Taylor Swift to guest star. Taylor is a nineteen-year-old country dynamo who writes all of her own songs and has won numerous awards for her soulful music. Taylor is a big fan of the Jonas Brothers and she was delighted to get the chance to work with them. She flew up to New York to spend some time with Kevin, Joe, and Nick before filming, and then shot her segments there. "I've had an awesome week; I've been in NYC shooting for the Jonas Brothers 3-D movie. It's been so much fun! We stayed right across from Central Park and I could see the whole city every time I looked out my window," Taylor Swift wrote in her personal blog. The guys became fast friends with Taylor, and she seems to really inspire them. And she should! After all, she broke into country music as a Sony/ATV staff songwriter when she was only fourteen years old. She could definitely relate to growing up in the spotlight, and she understands just how passionate the boys are about their music. Taylor's performance in the movie was just the feminine touch that it needed. When the boys saw the finished film for the first time, they were blown away. It was just what they had hoped to create and they couldn't wait for their fans to see it, too!

To wrap up the Burnin' Up tour, the Jonas Brothers performed three unbelievable shows at Madison Square Garden in New York City on August 9, 10, and 11. MTV filmed a ton of behind-the-scenes footage of the band plus the live performances for a special called *Jonas Brothers: Live & Mobile*. The MTV camera crews followed Kevin, Joe, and Nick from their hotel to the Hamptons, and even on their helicopter ride into the city! The boys answered questions from MTV viewers and talked about all of their most embarrassing moments. MTV even had a correspondent taking her own short videos and blogging about her experiences with the Jonas Brothers at www.mtv.com/specials/jonas-brothers-live/! The special was a hit with MTV viewers, and it was the first time the Jonas Brothers had gotten quite so much exposure on the famed music channel. The boys love all of the work they do with Disney, but they were also grateful for the opportunity to reach out to an even wider audience through MTV. All of the promoting the boys were doing was really paying off. Their fan base was growing, their concerts were becoming bigger and better, and the Jonas Brothers were ready to release their third and biggest album so far!

CHAPTER 14

BURNIN' UP

When Kevin, Joe, and Nick began looking at 2008 and what they wanted to accomplish that year, the number one thing on their list was to record and release their third album. The boys had been writing songs for their third album since the release of *Jonas Brothers*, so they had plenty of material to work with when they finally went into the studio. They worked with producer John Fields, with Jon Lind and Kevin Jonas Sr. serving as executive producers, and a number of experienced songwriters to tweak their sound until it was perfect.

The final album lineup included eight songs the boys had written and four songs they had cowritten. Kevin, Joe, and Nick were growing up and so was their sound. "The lyrical content has gotten more in-depth," Nick said on JonasBrothers.com. "It's about who we are as people and our personal lives, things we've gone through in the past 12 months." The album kicks off with "BB Good," a love song that Joe describes as "a big sing-along song, and it's fun," on JonasBrothers.com. The next track, "Burnin' Up," is the perfect summer party song. The Jonas Brothers even got their bodyguard, Big Rob, involved in that one by having him rap in the middle of the song! "It's about this girl," Joe stated on JonasBrothers.com. "Maybe she's at a party, and you feel that immediate connection. You both know it's there." But not all of the songs are as upbeat. Many of them deal with relationships gone wrong, breakups, and loneliness. Writing about those feelings probably helps Kevin, Joe, and Nick get over the pain of bad breakups or rejection. "'Shelf' is one [of] my favorite songs on the record," Nick stated on JonasBrothers.com. "Basically, it's about a girl that has a gallery of hearts."

But there is one song on the album that really stands out because it is about Nick's personal struggle with diabetes. Nick wrote the lyrics for *A Little Bit Longer* while he was struggling to accept his diagnosis. "I was having one of those days where I was discouraged. So I went into this empty hotel ballroom and wrote this song," Nick explained on JonasBrothers.com. Kevin and Joe were touched by the song, and they knew fans would respond and want to support Nick. "Nick sings this song every night and it brings people to tears. It's amazing," Kevin wrote on JonasBrothers.com.

The Jonas Brothers had no trouble deciding what to name the album: *A Little Bit Longer.* "A Little Bit Longer" was one of their favorite songs, and they felt like it was the perfect message to send to their fans. The Jonas Brothers were going to be around for longer than anyone had ever expected! The boys took their new material on tour, performing some of the songs at each show. Fans loved the new stuff, and became very eager for the third album to hit store shelves. But the Jonas Brothers had decided to release this album in a special way. They inked a special deal with iTunes that would allow fans access to the first four singles off of the album way before the album itself went on sale. Each song would also come with a special Jonas Brothers podcast.

On June 24, 2008, iTunes released the first single, "Burnin' Up," and it was followed on July 15, 2008, with "Pushin' Me Away." "Tonight" came next on July 29, 2008, and "A Little Bit Longer" was released on August 5, 2008. Each of the singles occupied the number 1 spot on iTunes for at least three days, and they helped make history when the Jonas Brothers became the first group ever to sell more than 100,000 digital downloads for three consecutive singles. And, when the album was finally released on August 12, 2008, it went straight to the number 1 spot on the Billboard 200 chart, selling 525,000 copies in its first week. It was the Jonas

Brothers' first number 1 album, and it was a huge accomplishment for the three brothers who had struggled for so long to make it in the music business! "We are just really living the dream right now," Kevin told the Associated Press. "For us, having this album finally hit stores and having [the fans] sing the songs, knowing that they can actually hear them and have it in their possession is the most amazing thing for us. We're so excited."

The boys were so motivated by the positive response to *A Little Bit Longer* that they got right to work on songs for their fourth album. They had a special bus on their Burnin' Up tour from Verizon that is actually a portable studio so that they could record new songs as soon as they wrote them! The Verizon Mobile Recording Studio has been used in the past by Pearl Jam, the Black Eyed Peas, Timbaland, and Madonna. The boys wrote and recorded most of the songs for their fourth album on the Burnin' Up tour, which is pretty cool. They could have been writing their next big hit while driving through your town! The boys actually pulled a lot of all-nighters on the tour working on the album, but it wasn't all work and no play. They also stayed up late a few nights just ordering burgers and playing Wii. Kevin, Joe, and Nick are hoping to polish the album and get it into stores as soon as possible in 2009, so fans won't have to wait too long for new Jonas songs!

CHAPTER 15

JONAS MANIA

As the Jonas Brothers became more popular, they began making more public appearances, much to the delight of Kevin, Joe, and Nick. Being in a famous rock group definitely has its advantages. The Jonas Brothers were invited to appear at places and events that they had never imagined they'd get to experience. They've been on talk shows, in parades, on award shows, and even put in a performance at the Miss Teen USA pageant!

One of the coolest places the Jonas Brothers have been to is the White House. They sang the National Anthem at the annual White House Easter Egg Roll in April 2007. And they were invited back to entertain visitors in June 2007 at the Celebrating

Women in Sports Tee Ball Game and Picnic on the White House's South Lawn. They opened the event with the National Anthem and sang some of their biggest hits at the picnic after the game. "A high point was being at the White House with the president," Joe told People.com. "He was so nice."

The boys were such a hit that they were invited back to perform again at the 2008 Easter Egg Roll. "We met the President and the First Lady," Joe told *Us Magazine*. "The president said he liked my shoes!" The boys were definitely making friends in high places! President Bush even invited the boys to attend the April 2008 White House Correspondents' Dinner at the Washington Hilton. "With our manners, my mom always told us, 'I'm training you for when you sit at the president's table,'" Joe told *Details*. "It's really paid off." Kevin, Joe, and Nick were the hit of the dinner when they arrived in tuxedos to find dozens of their Washington, D.C., fans waiting in front of the hotel. Even the president didn't get cheers like the Jonas Brothers!

But that was nothing compared to the response the boys got at the State Fair of Texas back in October 2007. When the band arrived at the local airport, traffic was too heavy for them to drive to the fair if they wanted to start their concert on time. So the boys took a helicopter ride over highways gridlocked with fans going to see them perform. Over 20,000 fans showed up for the Jonas Brothers' show that night. Only one other performer had ever had that kind of turnout, and that was Elvis Presley! "I thought, 'Wow, this is really awesome,'" Nick told People.com. "It was one of those moments where we just sat back in shock." And a month later, the boys appeared in the biggest parade in the country—the 81st annual Macy's Thanksgiving Day Parade. The boys had grown up watching the parade, so it was a big honor to be *in* it, especially since the boys all love Thanksgiving. They even have a family tradition of shouting "Gobble!" like a turkey whenever they cross a state line. How cute is that? Next the boys celebrated another major holiday tradition by performing "Hold On" and "S.O.S." on *Dick Clark's New Year's Rockin' Eve*. "It was the most unbelievable experience watching the ball drop," Kevin told People.com.

But by far some of the coolest experiences for the Jonas Brothers have been appearing on awards shows. The first show they did was the 2007 Teen Choice Awards in Los Angeles. They were nervous, but also very excited! They got dressed up in some seriously cool outfits and vintage sunglasses. "It's sunny out now so you gotta do the sunglasses," Nick told Tigerbeat.com. "It's part of the look." Kevin was actually sporting a brand-new hairstyle for the event. His normally straight locks were even curlier than Nick's. When it was their turn to present the award for Choice R&B Track, the boys took the stage, along with Miley, and announced that Sean Kingston was the winner for his hit single "Beautiful Girls." It was a great first awards show, but it was only a small taste of what was to come.

A few months later, Kevin, Joe, and Nick took the stage to perform at the American Music Awards at L.A.'s Nokia Theatre, but this time the show didn't go quite as planned! The night started out perfectly. The boys' manager even came in with a big surprise before the show. "[O]ur manager walked into the dressing room and told us that Celine Dion wanted to meet us! We walked to her dressing room, and when we got there she was so excited to meet us," the Jonas Brothers wrote on their MySpace page. Then the boys took the stage to perform "S.O.S." They had a supercool entrance planned with three panels of breakaway glass emblazoned with the bands' logo for the boys to jump through. But when Joe went through his glass, he tripped. "When the glass broke we started walking through," Joe wrote on the band's MySpace page. "On the way through I slipped and fell down on my hands and knees." He says seeing their fans smiling in the audience "let me know that I had to get right up and perform for them." Joe hopped right up and performed as if it had never happened, but he was hurt—he just hoped his fans didn't know it! "I had felt some pain but had no idea that there was so much blood," Joe wrote on MySpace. "I noticed that my white suit had blood on the knees. I also had cuts on my hand. We called the medic and they cleaned up my leg and hands." Even with the injury, it was an excellent night for the boys. "Beyoncé stopped us on our way back to our dressing room to let us know she thought we did great," the Jonas Brothers wrote on their MySpace page. "Akon spoke to us on our way out. He said he would love to work together. How amazing!" And after that performance, the Jonas Brothers' album sales doubled! "That," the boys' dad told *Rolling Stone*, "was huge." Joe got teased a lot for that fall. Ellen DeGeneres even presented him with a crash helmet with an attached microphone when the band appeared on her talk show, *The Ellen DeGeneres Show*, a few months later!

Appearing on awards shows was excellent,

but it was even cooler when the boys actually started being nominated for and winning awards! The Jonas Brothers won the 2007 Nickelodeon Kids' Choice Award for Favorite Music Group. And Perez Hilton, the famed celebrity blogger, presented the Jonas Brothers with his 2007 Perez Award for Hottest Teen Sensation on his show *What Perez Says*. In 2008, the boys really racked up the nominations. They were up for seven awards at the 2008 Teen Choice Awards, including Choice Breakout Group, Choice Male Red Carpet Style, Choice Hottie, Choice Music Single for "When You Look Me in the Eyes," Choice Music Love Song for "When You Look Me in the Eyes," Choice Summer Song for "Burnin' Up," and Most Fanatic Fans. They won all but Most Fanatic Fans. Nick told Usmagazine.com, "Last year we were here presenting, and to be back a year later and to be up for seven awards, that's really, *really* crazy! We are so blessed, and our fans are incredible, and we love it."

Kevin, Joe, and Nick were also nominated

for the 2008 Billboard Touring Award for Concert Marketing and Promotion and several international awards including the 2008 MTV VMA: Latin America awards for Best International Pop Artist, Best International New Artist, Best Fanclub, Song of the Year for "When You Look Me in the Eyes," and Best Ringtone for "When You Look Me in the Eyes"; and the 2008 TMF Awards in Belgium for Best New Artist, Best Pop, Best New Album for *Jonas Brothers*, and Best Video for "S.O.S."; and the 2008 Kids' Choice Awards of Italy for Best Band.

But the awards show the brothers were really psyched about for 2008 was the MTV Video Music Awards. They were nominated for Video of the Year for "Burnin' Up" and Pop Video of the Year, also for "Burnin' Up." They lost out on both awards to Britney Spears, but the boys were just fine with that. They were happy just to be nominated and they are huge Britney fans, so they were psyched just to meet her. "[W]e were so excited!" Kevin told Usmagazine.

com. "It is an honor and privilege to meet Britney Spears, of course. She looked great." Joe added, "We didn't want to become a 'Hi, Britney Spears, nice to meet you' and take a picture [type-of-thing]. I said, 'We have always loved your music,' and I told her she was the first CD I ever bought. She was like, 'Wow! Thank you.' She asked us how Big Rob [her famous old bodyguard] and Felicia [Culotta, Spears's former longtime personal assistant] were doing." In addition to meeting the princess of pop, the boys performed "Lovebug" in one of the biggest numbers of the night on the New York City-styled back lot at Paramount Studios. It was a huge hit on the show, and tons of viewers have watched the performance online since the show aired.

In addition to awards shows, Kevin, Joe, and Nick end up on television pretty regularly to give special performances or to do interviews on talk shows. The Jonas Brothers performed two songs at the 2007 Miss Teen USA pageant while the contestants modeled their evening gowns. The brothers had a lot of fun backstage flirting and consoling the girls that didn't make the cut to the final ten. Losing probably wouldn't be so bad with Kevin, Joe, and Nick there to cheer you up! In March 2008, the brothers were the special musical guests on NBC's hit show *Dancing with the Stars*. Fans really got into the performance. "[T]hey said it was one of the loudest audiences that they've ever had," Nick told People.com. Then in May 2008, they sat down with the entire family for a special interview with Oprah Winfrey! The boys even made it onto the *Tonight Show* with Jay Leno, where they performed "Burnin' Up" for an outdoor audience.

In August 2008, the boys had three iconic rock-and-roll moments that really blew them away. First, they were featured on the cover of *Rolling Stone* magazine, America's premiere music magazine and one of Kevin, Joe, and Nick's favorite reads. Next, the boys stopped by Madame Tussauds Wax Museum in Washington, D.C., for the unveiling of their very own wax figures. Only the coolest celebrities get wax figures made of them, but it was probably pretty strange seeing wax models of themselves. And a few days later, the boys hopped a plane to Cleveland, Ohio, to visit the Rock and Roll Hall of Fame. The band presented the suits and pants that they are wearing on the cover of *A Little Bit Longer* to Jim Henke, vice president of the Rock and Roll Hall of Fame. The suits became part of the *Right Here, Right Now!* exhibit, which included some of the hottest and most popular young artists. Being a part of a Rock and Roll Hall of Fame exhibit is a seriously big deal, and the boys were blown away by just how far they'd come since their early years pounding the pavement and trying to get noticed!

But not even the Rock and Roll Hall of Fame can compete in coolness to the response that the Jonas Brothers get at their concerts. Girls line up for hours before a show hoping to catch a glimpse of the Jonas cuties! "Never gets old," Joe told People.com.

"It's crazy when police have to hold back girls, but awesome." The boys were already on tour to support *A Little Bit Longer* when the album was released, so they got to experience the fan response firsthand at meet and greets before their shows. Fans couldn't wait to tell the Jonas Brothers exactly how much they loved the new album. And the boys wanted to meet each and every fan. At one show in Dallas, they met over four hundred fans in the 99-degree Texas heat! "They are the new music business—work hard, touch your fans," Brad Wavra, a Live Nation VP, told *Rolling Stone*. "We know a band that used to count the number in their meet-and-greets—if it was 50, and there were 51 people there, they wouldn't meet that 51st kid." The Jonas Brothers never care how long it takes, they love every single one of their fans and will do whatever it takes to make sure their fans know that. The boys love how excited the fans get. They've even seen lots of fans in red dresses and heels since that outfit was mentioned in "Burnin' Up"! There are always funny moments at meet and greets. "The dads make jokes like, 'Keep your hands off my daughter,'" Nick told *Rolling Stone*. "We've had some interesting situations with some fans, too—ones that will just come up and almost jump on you and be like, *'I love you, I love you!'*" Joe explained to *Details*. "I guess the only thing we'd be willing to say is, like, 'Thank you.' It's kind of awkward when they're like, *'Oh, you're so hot!'* How do you say anything to that?"

At the end of the day, the Jonas Brothers are willing to do just about anything for their fans. They know that they wouldn't be anywhere without them, so they make an extra effort to connect with fans whenever and however they can! They post YouTube videos on a special YouTube channel, respond to tons of fan mail, and update their MySpace page as regularly as possible. It's a full-time job, but the boys love every second of it. "[T]he minute we get onstage and feel the fans' energy," Kevin told People.com, "we know we can get through anything." Things just keep getting crazier, and life will never be the same for Joe, Nick, and Kevin, but that's okay with them. "We wake up every morning excited," Kevin told JonasBrothers.com, "because we get to do what we love." And, as a reminder of just how grateful they are to their fans for their success, the boys and their crew have a special ritual that they go through before every show. "We say, 'Living the dream, living the dream,'" Joe said to People.com. "And then we clap all the way to the stage." From the looks of it, the Jonas Brothers will be living the dream for years to come!

CHAPTER 16

BEHIND THE MUSIC

The Jonas Brothers' journey to the top has been wild! In a few short years, the boys have gone from a small band to superstars. But even with their busy careers, they still manage to have private lives.

So what do the boys do when they aren't performing? Well, like any teenage boys, they like to hang out with friends, flirt with girls, and just generally goof off. The brothers are also huge video-game fans. They each have their own Xbox Live account and they love to play anonymously with other gamers. "They have different gamer tags," David Henrie, a friend of the Jonas Brothers and one of the stars in *Wizards of Waverly Place*, told People.com. "People have no idea it's them." *Halo* is one of their favorites and they love having mini tournaments at their friends' houses! Kevin, Joe, and Nick can also often be found wrestling, dancing around to loud music, or jumping on their beds and sofas. All that horseplay is a great way for the brothers to get out excess energy before an event or show.

How else do they get pumped up before a show? "[W]e actually have a forty-five-minute lockdown where no one leaves and no one comes in. We get ready for the show, we change, get focused, play through all of the songs for that night on the acoustic guitar, do vocals, pray, push-ups, eat food," Kevin told Musicxcore.com. Getting pumped onstage is especially easy because the boys and their band have secret ways of communicating. "We give each other looks all the time where only we know what it means," Nick told *BOP*. "We could have an entire conversation with our band, and people will walk into our conversation and be like, 'What?'" Their band consists of John Taylor, who plays guitar and helps produce

Joe, Kevin, and Nick on the red carpet before the City of Hope benefit concert.

Nick, Kevin, and Joe team up with Demi Lovato and Miley Cyrus for a concert to benefit City of Hope.

The Jonas Brothers perform on ABC's *Good Morning America*.

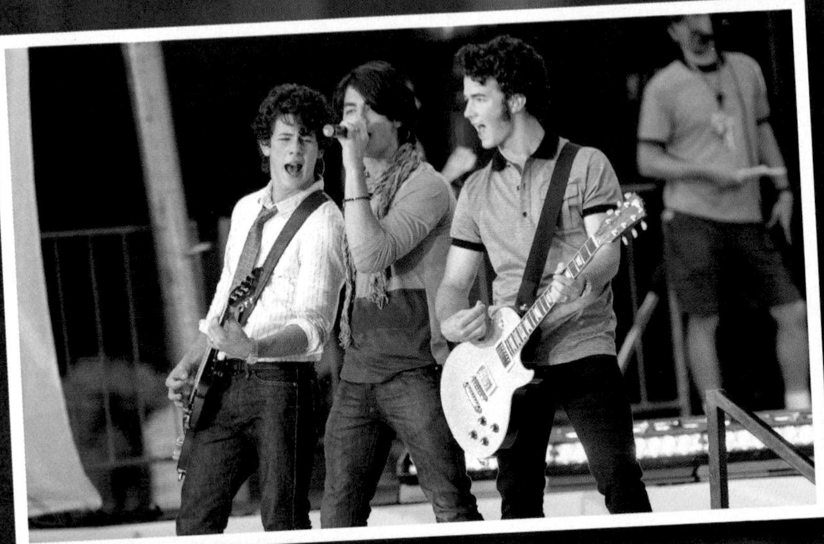

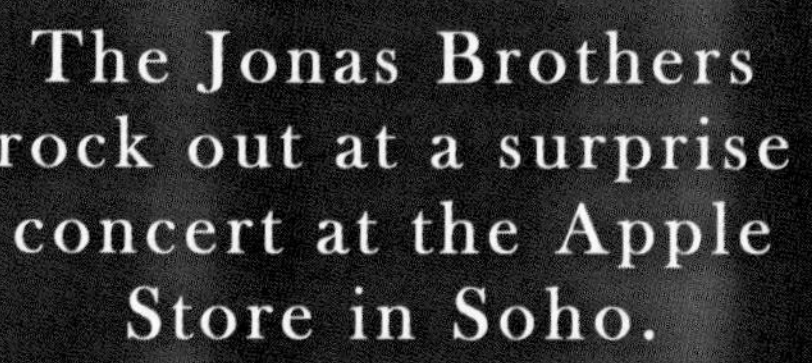

The Jonas Brothers rock out at a surprise concert at the Apple Store in Soho.

Nick

Joe

Kevin

Kevin, Nick, and Joe with Minnie and Mickey Mouse at the European premiere of *Camp Rock*.

The Jonas Brothers perform "Lovebug" at the 2008 MTV Video Music Awards.

The Jonas Brothers make an appearance on MTV's *Total Request Live.*

Kevin, Joe, and Nick pose with the wax figures of themselves at Madame Tussauds wax museum in Washington, D.C.

The Jonas Brothers shoot a music video with Taylor Swift in New York City.

Kevin and Taylor Swift

Nick

Joe

Nick, Joe, Kevin, and Frankie Jonas at the premiere of *Camp Rock*.

The Jonas Brothers with Vanessa Hudgens at the 2008 Teen Choice Awards.

Kevin, Joe, and Nick fly high while performing during the 2008 Teen Choice Awards.

many of the brothers' songs; Greg Garbowsky, a friend from New Jersey who has been playing bass guitar for the boys since the very beginning; Jack "Flawless" Lawless, who plays drums and percussion and joined the band in 2007; and Ryan Liestman on keyboards.

Kevin, Joe, and Nick spend a lot of time on their tour bus, and it's easy to get bored when stuck in such a small space for long periods of time. Luckily, the Jonas Brothers have twelve seriously sweet tour buses outfitted with comfy bunks, flat-screen TVs, computers, and different video game consoles! Nick starts his mornings off with schoolwork, then the boys work on new songs, give phone interviews, and handle other business-related stuff. But once that is all done, they have free time—and that's when the brothers sometimes get into trouble! They have a small video camera and they love to make funny videos of themselves that they will post on their YouTube or MySpace pages. Sometimes the boys will record fake talk shows or do celebrity impressions, and other times they will just film one another doing day-to-day stuff but add in funny commentary. Joe and Nick both especially love making videos, and they really ham it up when they're on camera.

Another favorite way they fill their downtime is by making prank phone calls! Kevin, Joe, and Nick have been known to prank-call all their friends, management team, publicists, and even other stars, like Aly and AJ Michalka of Aly & AJ. The boys' prank calls are usually pretty funny, and they are never mean. They'll pretend to be an angry parent whose daughter didn't win a Jonas Brothers contest or a fan desperate for info about the band. Luckily, most of the people they prank-call are amused by the boys' antics! The boys make plenty of serious phone calls, too, while on the road. They keep in touch with their friends all over the country with phone calls, texts, emails, and video chats.

Kevin, Joe, and Nick really are one another's best friends. Nick told *Rolling Stone*, "The good thing is that we have each other. On the road, Joe and I share a room, so we'll have conversations where we're in our beds and talk until 2:00 in the morning. We just have that relationship where we're really able to talk about anything." Their brotherly bond is especially strong, and working together has only made it stronger. "We just always have to remember that we're brothers before anything else. We're family," Kevin told Musicxcore.com. They do fight occasionally, but it's usually over silly stuff, and they always make up pretty quickly. "We're brothers and we are always going to have some quarrels. Nick always gets upset if I wear his socks. It is really funny," Joe told Scholastic.com during an interview. Kevin was quick to jump in, too. "We usually get along. We know we can't just get upset at each other and hold grudges against each other while we are onstage. It's not going to work." So what do they fight about? Clothes, lyrics when they are songwriting, and, of course, girls. "Because the girls we like are in between our ages," Kevin explained to

YM.com. Luckily, not even a beautiful girl can come between these brothers for too long! The strange thing is that a lot of people don't even realize that they really are brothers. "People seriously ask us all the time," Kevin told *Rolling Stone*. "'Are you guys really brothers?'" "It's like, no, we named our band Jonas Brothers just for fun," Joe added.

When Kevin, Joe, and Nick aren't on the road or working, they like to take time out at home. They just bought a huge house outside of Dallas, Texas, right on the edge of a golf course, and like to spend hours out on the green. "It's just like a random place to go on vacation," Kevin told *Rolling Stone*. "It doesn't even feel real. I get in a golf cart, go straight to the course. They're like, 'Hey, Mr. Jonas, you going to play today?' It's the best thing ever." But their home base these days is in Los Angeles. It was hard for the family to leave their little house in Wyckoff, New Jersey, where the boys grew up, but they needed to be in L.A. to take care of business. Their house in L.A. is huge compared to their home in New Jersey, where Kevin and Joe shared a bedroom, Frankie and Nick shared a bedroom, and all four brothers shared one bathroom! Now, each of the boys has his own room and plenty of space to play music and hang out. Their mom makes them all of their favorite Italian meals when they're home, including pasta and lasagna. And just like in any other family, they have to help with the cleanup after dinner—their chores include taking out the trash, doing the dishes, and setting the table. They love getting the chance to catch up with friends and just relax when they aren't on the road. "We like to play tennis, Wiffle ball, hang out with friends when we have the chance, and go see movies," Nick told *Time for Kids*.

Faith is a big part of the Jonas boys' personal lives. They don't perform Christian music, but all three boys have dedicated their lives to Christ. "On a personal level, faith is extremely important," Kevin Sr. told *Rolling Stone*. It's easy to see that their faith inspires them every day. Their favorite Bible verse is Matthew

5:14, "You are the light of the world. A city that is set on a hill cannot be hidden." Nick explained why the boys live by that verse to Musicxcore.com: "[I]t's really important for us because it's like there's a lot of bad things that go on, but we gotta be the light . . . [T]here's the band and there's all the success that comes with that, but in the midst of it all there's us being grounded and that's remembering where we're from." With that humble attitude, it's no surprise that the boys are on top. They don't take anything for granted. Lots of young stars get caught up in the trappings of fame and spend all of their time partying and posing for the paparazzi, but not the Jonas Brothers! They are committed to living a Christian lifestyle, which means they won't spend crazy nights in clubs, and they will never use drugs or alcohol. In addition to their personal moral convictions, the boys also have a strong support network of family and friends who help keep them grounded. "We're always keeping each other in check . . . and our mom and dad do, too. We have great parents, so even when we're playing shows in front of thousands of people, they still keep us grounded," Joe told Scholastic.com.

All three brothers wear promise rings on their left hands as reminders that they have pledged to remain pure until marriage. Those rings have caused some controversy in the media, but that hasn't stopped the boys from wearing them. And the styles of the rings are as different as the boys themselves, which makes sense since each boy's decision to wear a ring was very personal. "We all did it at one point in our life," Kevin told *Rolling Stone*. Kevin wears a punk-rock ring from Tiffany & Co. covered with studs. "It's pretty rock and roll," Kevin explained to *Details*. "It's getting banged up a little bit because of the guitar." Joe's ring is silver with a cross on it. "It actually ripped apart a little bit, just on the bottom, here, but I didn't want to get a new one, because this one means so much to me," Joe explained to *Details*. And Nick's ring is from one of his very favorite places in the whole world! "I got mine made at Disney World. It's pretty awesome," Nick told *Details*.

It's nice to know that there are boys out there who really value love, and every fan would probably love the chance to go on a date with one of the brothers! There have been tons of rumors about who the boys are dating, but Kevin, Joe, and Nick keep their lips sealed about their love lives. "It is our rule to not talk about our personal lives, especially who we are dating," the Jonas Brothers said on their MySpace page. "The same would be true if we were dating you." And the brothers are definitely open to dating a fan! "We have already dated fans or girls that are not celebrities. In fact, we really like to believe that the girl we will spend our lives with will be our biggest 'fan,'" the Jonas Brothers said on their MySpace page. Kevin, Joe, and Nick are really each just looking for a girl who can be their best friend, partner, and support system, and fame has nothing to do with that!

Even well-balanced, down-to-earth stars like

the Jonas Brothers enjoy some of the perks of being famous. "People give us free clothes to wear, which is really cool . . . I haven't actually purchased any clothes in about a year," Nick told *Popstar!* The free swag and glamorous events are fun, but for Kevin, Joe, and Nick the best part of being in a band is their fans. Nick loves being recognized by fans when he goes out, as he told Musicxcore.com. "Uh, it's cool. To tell you the truth it's kind of exciting because it's like you're working really hard and all of a sudden people recognize all of your hard work. It's a cool thing." Kevin agrees. "We're never like, 'Oh hi'; we're always like, 'HEY!' and give them hugs and stuff. It's cool, you know . . . It makes our day." Fans write on the brothers' MySpace page every day, leaving them encouragement and telling them how much they love their music.

The Jonas Brothers' fans are also really creative when it comes to getting the brothers' attention. They make amazing signs for concerts and give the brothers some really cool gifts. The boys say there are two gifts that have really stood out from the rest. The first is a model of the DeLorean, the time-traveling car from the *Back to the Future* movies. All three brothers love those movies, so the model was a great gift. The second gift that impressed the boys the most was a hippopotamus. Not a stuffed one or a figurine, but a real live hippo that lives on a wildlife preserve in Africa. The fan adopted the hippo, named it the Jonas Brothers, and then presented Kevin, Joe, and Nick with the certificate of adoption. "We were getting so many hippo gifts because we were doing that song 'I Want a Hippopotamus for Christmas.' We were getting like hippo pillows and, you know, hippos are the coolest things to get. But we looked and we were like, 'Oh cool, a picture of a hippo,' and they were like, 'No, that's your certificate, I got you a real hippo,'" Joe told Musicxcore.com. Now that's a creative gift!

Kevin, Joe, and Nick receive a lot of gifts from fans, but they also give a lot back. The boys consider themselves extremely blessed and they want to give back to those less fortunate whenever they can. And when they give, they do it in a *big* way! The Jonas Brothers earned about $12 million in 2007, and have donated 10 percent of their earnings to their charity, Change for the Children Foundation. Change for the Children Foundation is a foundation started by the Jonas Brothers that allows fans to donate to multiple children's charities including Nothing But Nets, American Diabetes Foundation, St. Jude Children's Research Hospital, Children's Hospital Los Angeles, and Summer Stars: Camp for the Performing Arts. The band told People.com that, "We started the Change for the Children Foundation to support programs that motivate and inspire children to face adversity with confidence, determination, and a will to succeed. And we think the best people to help children are their peers—kids helping other kids who are a little less fortunate."

For Nick, donating to children's hospitals is personal. Since his diagnosis with diabetes when he was thirteen, he's been very involved with diabetes charities. In August 2000, he partnered with Bayer Diabetes Care to become a diabetes ambassador. To fulfill those duties, Nick takes the time to reach out to kids with diabetes and teach them how to manage their illness. The boys also perform a number of concerts each year to benefit other charities and organizations, like the concert they did with Miley Cyrus, Demi Lovato, and Almost Amy to benefit cancer research and treatment programs at the Southern California-based City of Hope Hospital. The concert raised $1.2 million and Change for the Children Foundation donated an additional $250,000 on top of that! The Jonas Brothers are committed to making the world a better place in both their public and private lives, and nothing is sweeter than that!

CHAPTER 17

MORE JONAS BROTHERS TO COME

So what will the future hold for these hard-rocking brothers? The Jonas Brothers recorded their fourth album while touring to promote *A Little Bit Longer*, and will release it in 2009. They will continue touring as much as possible because bringing their music directly to their fans is their favorite part of being in a band. "Our next tour will be NEXT SUMMER . . . We will be going out for special performances throughout the year . . . The tour next year will be our first World Tour. We want to visit some of the areas where our music has done well, for example Latin and South America, Europe again, Asia, South Africa, Australia, and New Zealand," the Jonas Brothers wrote on their MySpace blog on

September 16, 2008. A holiday album might be in the works as well, especially since Christmas is their favorite holiday. "We wrote a holiday song, 'Girl of My Dreams,' and sang it at the Disney parade last year," Nick explained to E! Online. "It was a lot of fun . . . Maybe there is a holiday album in our future." That would be an awesome Christmas gift for any Jonas Brothers fan!

Their music will always come first for the Jonas Brothers. They are releasing their fourth album in 2009 and will get to work on their fifth shortly after that. But they do have some other projects that they would like to pursue. "[W]e would like to get into TV, movies, anything. We want to conquer all of it," said Kevin in an interview with the Jonas Brothers Street Team. The boys are already filming the television series *J*O*N*A*S* and the sequel to their smash hit made-for-television movie *Camp Rock*, both of which will premiere on the Disney Channel in 2009. In addition to television exposure, the boys would love to make it onto the big screen in some major motion pictures.

The boys are also on the lookout for ways to expand their musical horizons. They would love to do some duets with their favorite artists and their friends. They've already recorded one duet with Miley Cyrus, "We Got the Party," and they brought in their bodyguard Big Rob to do a rap in their song "Burnin' Up." There is also a chance that they could branch out from their signature pop-punk-rock sound and try something with a more hip-hop or R&B vibe. They've been in talks with hip-hop superstar Chris Brown to work with him. "I'm possibly doing something with them. If they want me on the record, I'll stay on the record, but I just wanted to write a record for those guys," Chris Brown told JustJared.com. Chris is a big Jonas Brothers fan, and Kevin, Joe, and Nick are looking forward to working with someone as innovative as Chris!

The boys also haven't completely given up

on the idea of doing some solo recording. Nick told *Rolling Stone* that he's considered recording under an alias. "It'd be great. Maybe even write songs under different names for other artists." The boys have already helped pal Demi Lovato out by writing and producing several of the songs on her debut album, *Don't Forget*, which hit store shelves on September 23, 2008, and they are very proud of how it turned out. Nick is even featured in Demi's first single, "Get Back." Kevin, Joe, and Nick would definitely like to do some more producing since working with other artists really inspires them for their own music. It's doubtful they'll have to wait long for the opportunity since there are plenty of singers out there who would love to record a Jonas Brothers song!

Kevin, Joe, and Nick are also looking forward to shooting more music videos with even cooler special effects. For the "Burnin' Up" video, they got their close friend Selena Gomez to guest star! The boys like bringing in close friends to give their videos that personal touch. And they love filming music videos with cool effects or a fun twist for fans to enjoy, like the video for "Hold On," which features wind so strong it almost blows them away!

The boys are also looking into launching their own fashion line. They already have supercool band T-shirts and merchandise for their fans to wear, but the boys would like to take their signature looks to the next level with a line of clothes for boys and girls. After all, they do have seriously cool style! "I'm not saying we're the best designers in the world, but being able to make what we like, that would be so cool," Kevin told E! Online. "We love dressing up and putting on different kinds of clothes." Guys everywhere are taking notice of the Jo Bros supercool looks and are starting to copy them. And what girl wouldn't want the chance to rock clothes that the Jonas Brothers had designed?

In addition to their work as a group, each brother has separate goals and dreams. All three boys would like to continue their education by attending college someday. Nick would like to return to Broadway at some point—since it combines all of his favorite things: a live audience, singing, and acting! But when he does return to the stage, he'd like to take on adult starring roles. Kevin would like to continue to pursue music and songwriting, and Joe has never completely given up on his dream of being a comedian.

No one can be certain exactly what the future holds, but the Jonas Brothers will be making music for the rest of their lives, whether they remain at the top of the charts or not. "The success is great," Nick told *Rolling Stone*. "But we wrote our last record while we were being dropped and playing for 10 people. We know what it's like to do it just for fun." Music will always be fun for the Jonas Brothers because they are truly passionate about it. With the support of all of their devoted fans, the Jonas Brothers will probably be successful for a long time to come!

CHAPTER 18

KEVIN

Since the Jonas Brothers are always together, it's sometimes easy to forget that they are individuals, but most fans have one brother that is their favorite! Girls who like the sweet, friendly type tend to like Kevin best. Kevin is the least flashy member of the band, but he's definitely the most charming! And he's also the glue that holds the band together, according to his brothers. Both Joe and Nick look to Kevin to keep them calm during hectic times. Kevin is extroverted and talkative and he loves getting to know new people. He is friends with every single person on each of the Jonas Brothers' tours and is always superfriendly with fans.

Kevin is very passionate and intense about

music, and even if he wasn't in the band, he'd probably be pursuing music on his own. It's so important to him that his worst fear is not being able to make music for the rest of his life! His Gibson Les Paul guitar is one of his most prized possessions, and he loves to just sit and play whenever he has something on his mind or when he needs a break from the world. "The moment I picked up a guitar, that was the minute I knew I wanted to do this for the rest of my life," Kevin told the *Kansas City Star*. But being a musician wasn't Kevin's first job. He used to mow lawns in his New Jersey neighborhood to make extra cash. Kevin likes to start every day by watching music videos on MTV (so he can keep tabs on the competition!) and drinking a huge cup of coffee. Kevin is a self-professed Starbucks addict, and swears he can smell Starbucks from a mile away!

Kevin has brown hair and brown eyes and he's worn glasses or contacts since he was little. He can wear his dark hair straight or curly, and he likes to switch it up often. Some little known facts about the oldest Jonas are that he is ticklish on his sides and that his favorite word is *excellent*—he even has his brothers saying it all the time! He also told People.com that he has "freckles in the form of a star" on his neck, and that the other kids made fun of his ears for being pointy when he was little. "They made fun of my Spock ears," Kevin told People.com. "I was such a dork."

Girls definitely don't think that Kevin is a dork anymore, but Kevin is slow to enter into relationships—he likes to make sure that a girl is right for him before he starts dating her. "The thing that attracts me to a girl most: self-confidence," Kevin told *Teen* magazine. Kevin also loves a girl with a great sense of style! Once Kevin does find the perfect girl for him, he is very devoted. He likes to stay connected with lots of emails, IMs, and phone calls. When Kevin wants to impress a girl, he has one fail-safe way of letting her know how he feels—he'll get his brothers to help him write her a song! "We'll put it out there pretty obviously," Kevin told *BOP*.

And once he scored a date with a special girl, Kevin had the perfect date all planned out according to briomagazine.com in an article from when he was still a Jersey boy. "We live in Wyckoff, New Jersey, so I believe the best date would be going to New York City and having dinner. A restaurant we like is La Mela. Tables are set up in the street covered with overhanging lights. Then head to a Broadway show." Even back on his very first date, Kevin was pretty smooth. "I went to a little candlelit restaurant in New Jersey, and it was really cute," Kevin told *J-14*. "After dinner, we went and saw Christmas lights. It was awesome. It was a good first date." What a romantic! Kevin even has part of his life with his future wife planned out. "When I get married and have kids, I want to have a daughter named Madison Grace," Kevin told *Teen* magazine.

Kevin's fans think he's pretty suave, but he has had his share of embarrassing moments. "I've fallen off the stage before," Kevin told the sptimes.

com. "[I]t had a catwalk-ish area and I didn't see that I was stepping out beyond it and I just kind of fell off the stage. I landed properly and then jumped back up and tried to play it off like I meant to do it. But I definitely did not mean to do it." Kevin can have some not-so-smooth moments, like accepting gross dares from his brothers. "I'm an adventurous eater and I'll try anything once; one time I even ate fish eyes!" Kevin told *Teen* magazine. And, like a lot of guys, Kevin is really into cars. He has a "Jeep Commander. Leather seats, black on black; only way to roll," as he told Musicxcore.com. But Kevin is also very concerned about the environment, so he spends most of his time driving his Chevrolet Tahoe 2 Mode Hybrid SUV. The SUV looks cool and it's good for the planet! But whether he's eating some exotic dish or just cruising around his neighborhood, Kevin always looks good doing it!

KEVIN FAST FACTS

FULL NAME: Paul Kevin Jonas II

NICKNAME: Kev

DATE OF BIRTH: November 5, 1987

PLACE OF BIRTH: Teaneck, New Jersey

HEIGHT: 5' 9"

HOBBIES: Playing guitar and bowling

INSTRUMENTS: Guitar

FAVORITE FOOD: Sushi

FAVORITE COLOR: Green

FAVORITE ICE CREAM: Rocky Road (especially with cookie dough and hot chocolate sauce)

FAVORITE SPORT: Pole vaulting

FAVORITE MOVIE: *About a Boy*

LUCKY NUMBER: Fifteen

IF HE WASN'T A MUSICIAN, HE'D LIKE TO BE: A race car driver

ARE YOU KEVIN'S TYPE? TAKE THIS *QUIZ* TO FIND OUT.

1. On a date you:
a. text your friends how it's going every twenty minutes!
b. turn your phone off before the date so you can focus only on him.

2. You love it when your crush shows up to surprise you, even if you haven't done your hair or makeup yet.
a. No
b. Yes

3. Boys you like are always:
a. casual and funny.
b. sweet and romantic.

4. For a casual afternoon with your guy, you'd rather:
a. hang out and watch a baseball game.
b. go shopping at the mall and have coffee.

5. Do you like to spend hours chatting with your boyfriend on the phone or on IM?
a. No, you aren't much of a phone person.
b. Yes, of course!

6. If your boyfriend is friendly with other girls, do you get jealous?
a. Yes!
b. No, you know he only has eyes for you.

7. You would describe yourself as a:
a. tomboy.
b. girly girl.

8. Your perfect date with your crush would be:
a. a date with a group of your friends to the movies or the fair.
b. an intimate dinner at a romantic restaurant.

If you answered mostly As, then Kevin probably isn't your perfect match. You and Kevin would be great as friends and you'd have a lot of fun hanging out together, but there is probably not much romantic chemistry there. However, you never know, since sometimes opposites attract!

If you answered mostly Bs, then Kevin would be the perfect date for you! You are a romantic at heart and you like a sweet, romantic guy who loves to stay connected and is full of surprises. You are as into fashion as Kevin is and you love looking cute for your guy! And Kevin would love your confidence and sweet nature.

CHAPTER 19

JOE

Girls who love to laugh will usually claim Joseph as their favorite Jonas brother, since he has a reputation for being totally hilarious. Joe wanted to be a comedian when he grew up, and he hasn't completely given up on that dream. He'd love to host *Saturday Night Live* some day and have the chance to participate in some of their famous comedic sketches. He's the one that usually suggests the boys make prank phone calls, goofy YouTube videos, or give silly answers during interviews. But most fans don't know that Joe actually used to be shy when he was little. He's since grown out of it and now he's totally outgoing and fun!

Joe gets teased a lot by his brothers for being

really concerned with his appearance. He takes the longest to get ready in the morning and is constantly borrowing his brothers' clothes, shampoo, moisturizer, and hair gel. "I take things from Kevin's closet, maybe a little from Nick," Joe laughingly told Tigerbeat.com. He starts every day with a long run because staying in good shape is very important to Joe. He has a personal trainer in Los Angeles and drinks Muscle Milk to help bulk up! Even when the boys are on tour, he'll find a way to get in his workouts. Joe is the only one of the brothers who really knows how to cook, and his specialty is breakfast. He loves to prepare bacon, sausage, chocolate chip pancakes, and omelets, but his favorite breakfast food is Pop-Tarts.

Joe doesn't usually get embarrassed. He loves to be in the spotlight, but he has had a few moments that made him blush. "One time I had a hole in my pants like the entire show and I didn't realize until like after the meet and greet and I got back and I sit down and I'm like, 'Oh man!' It was really embarrassing," Joseph told Musicxcore.com. Or the time he fell onstage at the 2007 American Music Awards! Luckily his fans' support helped him get over it.

Joe is definitely girl-crazy and there have been a lot of rumors about who he's dated or is interested in dating. In August 2008, tabloids began guessing that Joe was dating country superstar Taylor Swift. They were right. Joe and Taylor kept quiet on the subject, but they were spotted together in New York City, and Joe took time off of his busy schedule to attend one of Taylor's concerts. Joe told Ryan Seacrest on his KIIS-FM radio show that "I think anyone would be lucky to be dating her." The two have since broken up, and Taylor was heartbroken. She even wrote a song about it for her latest album *Fearless*. How could anyone not be bummed after losing a boy like Joe?

Joe has since been rumored to be dating actress Camilla Belle, who starred in the Jonas Brothers' music video for "Lovebug." Joe has dated some high-profile girls in the past, including AJ of Aly & AJ and

Mandy, who he made famous with the Jonas Brothers song "Mandy." Joe thinks it's great that his fans are interested in who he's dating, and he understands why they care. "I get it. When I was young, I wanted to know what my favorite bands were up to all the time," Joe told *Rolling Stone*.

Joe's ideal girl would be someone warm and funny who knows how to have a good time and who doesn't take life too seriously. Joe told *Teen* magazine that he likes to make a girl laugh if he's interested in her by using a silly pick-up line on her like, "You're like my library card, 'cuz I'm checkin' you out." One of the best dates Joe ever went on was on Halloween. "I bought this huge costume to make my crush laugh," he told *TWIST*. "I was dressed up as a cowboy riding a bull. I liked it because it had this button. When you pressed it, the cowboy suit blew up and became really huge! She dressed up as a milkshake. It was really, really awesome! We went trick-or-treating all day." So if you want to impress Joe, all you have to do is be easygoing and make him laugh.

Joe recently graduated from high school, and his tutor gave him a special graduation ceremony onstage at a concert in Atlanta. He got to wear a cap and gown and everything! Joe's favorite book is *A Wrinkle in Time* by Madeleine L'Engle and he also loves the *Narnia* series by C.S. Lewis. Joe is definitely one smart cookie, but he also loves sports and he has a dangerous side. For his nineteenth birthday, Joe got a motorcycle with a sidecar from his family! "I'm pumped!" Joe said in an interview with Radio Disney. "Don't worry," added Kevin, "there were lots of helmets given." And Joe channels some of music's biggest bad boys when he's performing. "On stage I've kind of studied Mick Jagger and things like that and really have been influenced by him and his persona on stage," Joe was quoted on Usmagazine.com. Joe is usually the Jonas brother who really works the crowd during concerts, so he works hard to be charismatic and fun to watch. Joe loves the way Mick Jagger owns the stage, as Joe explained to *Rolling Stone*. "I'm really inspired by Mick Jagger and

Freddie Mercury—the big frontmen." Joe is definitely the ham out of the group, whether the boys are just hanging out or rockin' out. But it's his hilarious antics and funny jokes that make him so lovable to his fans!

JOE FAST FACTS

FULL NAME: Joseph Adam Jonas
NICKNAMES: Joe or Danger
DATE OF BIRTH: August 15, 1989
PLACE OF BIRTH: Casa Grande, Arizona
HOBBIES: Making movies, jogging, and working out
INSTRUMENTS: Guitar, piano, percussion (tambourine)
FAVORITE MOVIES: *Finding Neverland* and *The Four Feathers*
FAVORITE FOOD: Chicken cutlet sandwich with mayo
FAVORITE CAKE: Strawberry shortcake
FAVORITE COLOR: Blue
FAVORITE ICE CREAM: Chocolate marshmallow (especially with peanut butter mixed in)
FAVORITE SPORT: Wiffle ball
FAVORITE ACTOR: Johnny Depp
FAVORITE SUBJECT: Math
IF HE WASN'T A MUSICIAN, HE'D LIKE TO BE: A comedian

ARE YOU JOE'S TYPE? TAKE THIS QUIZ TO FIND OUT.

1. Do you like surprises?
a. Yes, I love them.
b. No, I like to plan ahead.

2. If your crush wanted to pull a (harmless!) practical joke on someone, you would:
a. help him do it.
b. worry that it would hurt the person's feelings.

3. Boys you like are always:
a. the life of the party.
b. a little shy and mysterious.

4. For a casual afternoon with your guy, you'd rather:
a. watch a hilarious movie.
b. go for a long walk and talk.

5. If you do something embarrassing on a date, you would:
a. make a joke about it and laugh it off.
b. freak out and leave as quickly as possible.

6. To catch the attention of your crush, you would:
a. jump into a dance-off and show off your best and funniest moves!
b. bake him some cookies and write him a sweet note.

7. You would describe yourself as a:
a. laid-back girl who can go with the flow.
b. planner who likes things just so.

8. If your date showed up for the school dance wearing a vintage powder-blue tux, you would:

a. love it—it matches your disco dress perfectly!

b. be a little embarrassed that he wasn't dressed like everyone else.

If you answered mostly As, then Joe is the Jonas for you. You both love being the center of attention and laughing. You enjoy spending time with your boyfriend one-on-one, but you also love going bowling, playing mini-golf, or racing go-carts with a big group of friends. You are known for your sense of humor and you are just fine with making plans on the go.

If you answered mostly Bs, then Joe and you might be better as friends. Joe loves to be the life of the party, but you prefer to spend more time alone with your guy. Joe would definitely make you laugh with his goofy jokes, but you also like a guy who is more sensitive. But you never know, you might be just the girl to turn Joe into a romantic!

CHAPTER 20

NICK

The youngest member of the band, Nick, is the favorite of romantic girls everywhere. Nick has a reputation for being sweet, sensitive, and a hopeless romantic. Nick is quick to fall for girls, and many of the Jonas Brothers' songs are the result of just that, as he told *BOP*. "When I really have inspiration for something, it's really easy for me to write a song." Girls definitely inspire Nick! He's been pretty quiet about his love life, but recently Miley Cyrus confirmed that she and Nick dated for two years. "There was a point in our lives when we were very close," Nick told *Rolling Stone*. "We were neighbors when we were on tour together. It was good. Just really close." The relationship didn't work out because the two had such crazy schedules that they just never got to spend any time together. "Nick and I loved each other," Miley said to *Seventeen*. "We *still* do, but we were *in love* with each other. For two years he was basically my 24/7. But it was really hard to keep it from people. We were arguing a lot, and it really wasn't fun." But they remain close friends to this day.

Since then, rumors have been swirling that Nick is dating Selena Gomez, star of the Disney Channel's *Wizards of Waverly Place*. Selena Gomez told Ryan Seacrest on his KIIS-FM show, "Well, he's an amazing guy, Ryan. Anybody would be very lucky to be dating him." They've been spotted together at lots of events and they both admit to being close friends. Nick and Selena would definitely make a cute couple, but if things don't work out with Selena, Nick will be on the hunt for a special kind of girl. "She has to be kinda quiet, like a serious person—totally driven. People say I'm competitive, but I consider myself to be very driven," Nick told YM.com. He explained to briomagazine.com that if he was planning the perfect date, he "would buy box tickets to a Yankees' game [for him and his date] and watch the Yankees beat the Red Sox."

Nick is a total sports nut! "My favorite sport is baseball, and I love the New York Yankees and Derek Jeter," Nick told *Teen* magazine. Now that the boys live in Los Angeles, Nick doesn't get to see his team play as often as he would like. Luckily, Nick is also a fan of the L.A. Dodgers. He even celebrated his sixteenth birthday at their stadium. "[Kevin, Joe, and Nick] rented out the stadium last night to play a baseball game with some friends," a source told E! Online. Nick and at least fifteen of his closest friends hung out at the stadium for a few hours in baseball gear from Big 5 Sporting Goods. Sounds like a pretty fun birthday party! Nick always makes sure to visit local baseball stadiums when he can while on tour. He's been to lots of them and he and his brothers even got to participate at batting practice at Busch Stadium in

St. Louis, Missouri. Nick was the best batter by far! But Nick also loves to play golf. He and Joe hit the green every chance they get!

According to his brothers, Nick takes the longest to wake up in the mornings and starts every morning with a big breakfast and some quality time with his guitar. He prefers to write music in the mornings, when his mind is at its freshest. His favorite guitar is his red Gibson SG and his favorite Jonas Brothers song is "Please Be Mine" since it was the first song the boys ever wrote together—plus it's a soulful, romantic ballad and those are Nick's favorites! Nick is definitely the heart of the group, and he knows how to really touch his fans emotionally. He is also the most mature Jonas Brother, even if he is the youngest in the band. "People call me an 'old soul,'" Nick was quoted on Usmagazine.com. "It's a nice way to say that I'm like an old man. When I was 3, I acted like I was 30. Now I act like I'm 50. I get made fun of a lot, but it's all good. It's who I am." Nick even likes music from another generation, like the soulful tunes of Stevie Wonder or country classics from Johnny Cash. Nick would love to do a Jonas-Cash tribute album. "We could call it, *Jonas Brothers Pay Tribute to the Man in Black*," he told *Rolling Stone*.

Some things about Nick that most fans might not know are that he is a neat freak when it comes to keeping his closet organized, he still wears a retainer at night, and he is ticklish right above his knees. Nick also has a secret talent. "I can do one-handed cartwheels," Nick told *Teen* magazine. And Nick is picky about his food. "My mom points out that I eat my hamburgers in a weird way—I eat all around the edges, in a circle, instead of eating them straight through," Nick told *Teen* magazine. He is also addicted to green tea Frappuccinos from Starbucks! Nick's most embarrassing moment on tour happened when he fell during a performance. "I fell onstage once . . . into our guitar player . . . I was kind of just like I better keep it down a bit because I was really rocking out and

I just fell," Nick told Musicxcore.com.

And don't be jealous, but Nick does have a serious love in his life. It's the golden retriever puppy named Elvis that Nick got for his sixteenth birthday. He named the adorable puppy for two of his favorite musicians—Elvis Costello and Elvis Presley. It looks like the Jonas boys will be adding a doggie bed to their tour bus! He's sweet, soulful, and an animal lover—it's no wonder his fans love him so much!

NICK FAST FACTS

FULL NAME: Nicholas Jerry Jonas

NICKNAME: Nick or Nicky (but only to his family!)

DATE OF BIRTH: September 16, 1992

PLACE OF BIRTH: Dallas, Texas

HEIGHT: 5' 6"

HOBBIES: Music, songwriting, baseball, collecting baseball cards, tennis, golf

INSTRUMENTS: Guitar, drums, piano

COLLECTION: Baseball cards

FAVORITE HOLIDAY: Thanksgiving

FAVORITE FOOD: Steak

FAVORITE SNACK: Twinkies

FAVORITE DESSERT: Pumpkin pie

FAVORITE CANDY: Gummy worms

FAVORITE MUSICIANS: Stevie Wonder and Johnny Cash

FAVORITE MOVIES: *Finding Neverland* and *Better Off Dead*

FAVORITE COLOR: Blue

FAVORITE ICE CREAM: Cotton candy

FAVORITE SPORT TO WATCH: Baseball

FAVORITE SPORT TO PLAY: Golf

IF HE WASN'T A MUSICIAN, HE'D LIKE TO BE: A professional golfer or baseball player

ARE YOU NICK'S TYPE? TAKE THIS QUIZ TO FIND OUT.

1. If your boyfriend gave you a necklace for a gift, you would:
a. wear it on special occasions.
b. never take it off!

2. Your crush is:
a. the class clown.
b. mysterious, sensitive, and a total sweetie.

3. Your perfect date would be:
a. going to a party with all of your friends.

b. a walk on the beach and a romantic dinner.

4. For a casual afternoon with your guy, you'd rather:
a. hang out at the park.
b. watch a great baseball game.

5. You always know exactly what you want, and you always go for it!
a. False
b. True

6. You would describe yourself as a:
a. tomboy who loves to have a good time.
b. focused lady.

7. The most romantic night you can think of would include:
a. you and your date at your favorite band's concert.
b. dinner, dancing, and the perfect good-night kiss.

8. Do you tell your boyfriend all of your deepest, darkest secrets?
a. No, you like to keep some things to yourself.
b. Yes, you are completely open when you are in love.

If you answered mostly As, then you and Nick might not be a match right off the bat. He's super-romantic, while you are more laid-back. Nick can be really intense when he's in a relationship, but you are more casual. But that might not be a bad thing. Nick has been linked with Miley Cyrus and Selena Gomez, both of whom are known for being tomboys who are independent and laid-back, so you might be just the girl for him!

If you answered mostly Bs, then you and Nick are a perfect match. You both love being in love and can't wait to find the perfect person for you. You would appreciate his romantic side, and he would love that you like to chill out and watch sports every once in a while. Nick would love having you to confide in and you would appreciate all the little things he would do to show you how much he loves you! Plus you are both driven and always go after what you want.

CHAPTER 21

FRANKIE

The youngest Jonas is still a little bit of a mystery to many of the Jonas Brothers' fans. His name is Franklin Nathaniel Jonas, but he goes by Frankie to his friends and family. He was born on September 28, 2000, in Wyckoff, New Jersey.

Frankie is just as into music as his big brothers are. Frankie thinks his brothers' fans are supercool and he's very proud of his big brothers for inspiring so many people. He's happy to be there to support his brothers as they pursue their dreams. Since the entire Jonas family travels together, Frankie is used to life on the road. He is homeschooled to make sure he keeps on track with his education. He gets to see lots of cities across the county, and since he isn't the one performing he actually gets to do a little sightseeing! Frankie is one of the biggest fans of Kevin, Joe, and Nick's music. His favorite song off the *Jonas Brothers* album is "That's Just the Way We Roll," but Frankie has seen so many Jonas Brothers concerts that he doesn't really watch anymore. Frankie does love hanging out backstage. To kill time waiting around for shows to start, Frankie told People.com, "[I] ride my scooter up and down the halls fast, and I play computer games." It isn't all fun and games, though. Frankie has learned a lot about the music business from being on tour with his brothers!

Frankie has performing in his blood. In fact, he already has his own band! "I already have a band. It's called Webline. I've already written a bunch of songs. It's pretty awesome," Frankie told People.com. Nick often helps Frankie polish his songs, and Frankie considers Nick to be his best friend. The band has changed names a few times from Hollywood Shake Up to Drop/Slap to Rock Slap to Webline. But one thing

Frankie is sure of is that his band is going to be even bigger than the Jonas Brothers, as he explained to People.com. "My brothers will be the opening act for my band!" Frankie wants to become a pro at drums, guitar, and piano, and write all of his own music. But it will probably be a little while before Frankie is old enough to really rock out!

Frankie has more in common with Kevin, Joe, and Nick than just music—he's also a promising actor and comedian. Frankie is going to have a small role in *Camp Rock 2*, and he is starring alongside his brothers in their new television show *J*O*N*A*S*. Frankie has no shame when the cameras are following, and is willing to do whatever it takes to get a laugh onscreen. He really got into acting by appearing with Kevin, Joe, and Nick in their homemade YouTube videos. The videos are totally goofy and funny, and fans have really responded to Frankie's crazy antics online. He definitely gives his brothers a run for their money in terms of star power!

But even Frankie doesn't perform all of the time. He's a huge sports nut who plays football and baseball and loves the New York Yankees. In fact, Frankie was the star center for his football team, the Jr. Hornets. He also loves cartoons, and told People.com that he can't live without "TV, because it mesmerizes me." He also has a large collection of Webkinz toys and loves the color red-orange. Fans often refer to Frankie as the Bonus Jonas, but his family calls him Frank the Tank. Frankie thinks his nickname is pretty cool, as he told People.com. "I have it engraved on a brass ring I got at Disney World." It can be difficult for Frankie to maintain friendships since he isn't in one place very long. Luckily, Frankie has made a few friends who understand his crazy lifestyle. While hanging out on the set of *Hannah Montana* and *Camp Rock* with his brothers, Frankie became friends with up-and-coming stars his own age like Miley Cyrus's sister Noah and Demi Lovato's sister Madison. He keeps in touch with his friends using video chats and lots of text messages!

Frankie is a tough, cool, and totally fun kid who is well on his way to being just as awesome as his older brothers. So keep an eye out for what Frankie does next because he's sure to take the Jonas name to the next level as he gets older.

FRANKIE FAST FACTS

FULL NAME: Franklin Nathaniel Jonas

NICKNAMES: Frankie or Frank the Tank

DATE OF BIRTH: September 28, 2000

PLACE OF BIRTH: Wyckoff, New Jersey

HOBBIES: Riding his bike, playing video games, and watching TV

INSTRUMENTS: Guitar, but he's learning how to play drums

FAVORITE SPORT: Baseball

FAVORITE SPORTS TEAM: New York Yankees

FAVORITE COLOR: Red-orange

FAVORITE HOLIDAY: Christmas

FAVORITE TOYS: Webkinz and LEGOs

FAVORITE TV SHOW: *The Suite Life of Zack & Cody*

CELEBRITY FRIENDS: Noah Cyrus, Miley Cyrus's sister, and Madison De La Garza, Demi Lovato's little sister

WHAT HE WANTS TO BE WHEN HE GROWS UP: A musician, just like his brothers!

CHAPTER 22

JONAS STYLE

The Jonas Brothers have serious rock star style! Most teenage boys think dressing up means putting on clean jeans and a polo shirt, but not Kevin, Joe, and Nick! They love fashion and they are very particular about their clothing. The band has a distinct, signature style, but each of the brothers has their own personal style that sets them apart as individuals.

The boys have been interested in fashion for a long time, and when they first started out as performers they chose all of their own clothing. These days, however, the boys are way too busy to shop for themselves! Instead, they have a fantastic stylist named Michelle Tomaszewski who keeps them looking cool and put together at all times. But Michelle didn't create the Jonas look. She takes her cues from what the boys are already wearing. "We love a lot of different designers," Kevin told the *Virginian Pilot*. "We all wear different things, like J. Lindeberg, Dior, Phillip William. We really do pay attention to what we wear, but we have a stylist. We work alongside her because we are extremely busy. So having the ability to even go shopping is an issue. So we're able to pick the clothes we like when she brings them to us." It must be nice not to have to scour the mall for the perfect outfit!

They Jonas boys are very inspired by styles from the 1970s and 1980s. They love skinny jeans, skinny ties, fitted shirts and blazers, and funky sneakers and boots. When the band performs, they like to dress in tailored suits and dress shirts with a vintage feel in light colors, so that it's easy for fans to see them onstage! For more casual shows, the boys tend to rock out in vintage T-shirts, colorful skinny jeans, and sneakers. And for red carpet occasions, the Jonas Brothers really amp things up! They choose preppy blazers and trousers, vintage-inspired three-piece suits, or leather ensembles that are truly rock-star chic. The Jonas Brothers are so stylish as a band because they aren't afraid to take risks and try new things. They love bright colors and trying out new cuts and accessories. With their good looks, confidence, and charisma, the Jonas Brothers can get away with wearing just about anything, but the boys always take the time to make sure they look their very best for their fans whether at a casual meet and greet or headlining an arena tour. Their style continues to evolve and change along with their music, and their fans are definitely looking forward to seeing where it takes them next!

Part of what makes the Jonas Brothers' style so cool is how diverse it is. Each of the boys has his own distinct look, so there's something for every type of fan to appreciate about their fashion sense. Kevin has a very laid-back, urban style. He loves dark, skinny jeans or leather pants and boots with slightly pointed toes.

He likes to layer Ts with button down shirts and vests or cool cropped jackets. He also likes to mix things up by adding scarves and ties or cool hats to finish off his look. Kevin is very inspired by the fashion trends that can be found on the streets in the most artistic neighborhoods of Brooklyn and Manhattan. Kevin has naturally curly hair that he keeps fairly long, but he has been known to straighten it in the past for a different look.

Joe, in contrast, has the wildest and most colorful fashion sense of all of the brothers. He loves bright, neon colors like hot pink, bright green, and electric yellow, and buys his skinny jeans in every color of the rainbow. He loves 1980s vintage T-shirts or retro-inspired T-shirts with funny slogans and graphics on them, and fitted blazers with funky trimming and modern cuts. He is also big on sneakers with graphic patterns and fun sunglasses. He straightens his black hair every day to achieve his signature hairstyle, and he uses a lot of hair gel, hair wax, and hairspray to keep it in place!

Nick has the preppiest style out of all of the brothers. He wears a lot of button-down and polo shirts and likes to wear nautical-inspired blazers with the sleeves rolled up. Like his brothers, Nick loves jeans, but he has also been spotted in khaki pants and traditional, preppy gold clothes for when he's out on the green on his days off. Nick does like to mix things up from time to time and pair his jeans with snap-front western-style plaid shirts! Nick never straightens his naturally curly brown hair, which all of his fans appreciate since he is so well known for those curls!

It's pretty easy for boys to score the Jonas look. Stores like Urban Outfitters, Forever 21, and H&M carry skinny jeans, button-down shirts with fun prints, and vintage-inspired T-shirts that look a lot like the clothes that Kevin, Joe, and Nick wear every day. Since girls can't go out and buy exactly what the Jonas Brothers are wearing, they have to get a little more creative. Fans inspired by Kevin can wear skinny black leggings with flat boots, a long-sleeve tee, a menswear-style vest, and a cool printed scarf. Joe fans can take an oversized 1980s-style T-shirt and wear it over neon tights as a fun dress with funky sneakers. And girls who love Nick best can wear a cute fitted polo or western-style shirt with a jean skirt and a fun blazer to look like their favorite star!

Want to know which Jonas Brother you have the most in common with style-wise?

TAKE THE QUIZ BELOW TO FIND OUT!

1. You are going to a movie with friends, and you wear:
a. jeans, an old T-shirt, and cool Converse sneakers.
b. leggings, a long-sleeve dress, and a hand-knit scarf.
c. a khaki skirt, preppy flats, and a cute button-down top.

2. It's the first day of school and you really want to stand out. What do you wear?
a. A brightly colored dress with funky 1980s-style booties
b. Skinny jeans, a white T-shirt, a tweed vest, and brown suede boots
c. A cute pleated skirt and a polo shirt with puffy sleeves

3. You have a date with your crush and you want to look perfect! What is your style for the night?
a. Fun and funky
b. Cool and sophisticated
c. Preppy and sweet

4. How long do you spend getting ready every morning?
a. About an hour and a half
b. At least an hour
c. Thirty minutes

5. For the prom, you would choose:
a. a short dress with a fun, full skirt in a bright color.
b. a long, elegant black dress with funky accessories.
c. a short, slinky red dress and high heels.

6. Your favorite store is:
a. your local thrift store.
b. Forever 21.
c. Abercrombie & Fitch.

7. To head to the beach for the summer, your bathing suit is a:
a. bikini in a fun, girly print.
b. retro-inspired one-piece suit.
c. ruffled bikini in a girly plaid.

8. Your favorite accessory is a:
a. pair of white plastic sunglasses.
b. bohemian printed scarf.
c. chunky chain necklace.

9. Your favorite fashion icon is:
a. Selena Gomez
b. Demi Lovato
c. Taylor Swift

10. If you could describe your fashion sense in one word, it would be:
a. bright!
b. funky
c. classic

If you chose mostly As, your style is most like Joe's. You have a big personality and love to stand out in a crowd and your fashion reflects that. You love bright colors, bold graphic designs, and having fun with fashion!

If you chose mostly Bs, your style is most like Kevin's. You never follow the crowd and like your style to have a funky, urban, rock-and-roll edge that is a little artsy and eclectic. You like to acquire unique pieces and use them to jazz up plainer outfits!

If you chose mostly Cs, your style is most like

Nick's. You like to look polished and put together and you love preppy details like ribbons, pearls, and plaids. Your wardrobe is stocked with classics like the perfect black or red dress, nice jeans, and button-down tops!

CHAPTER 23

THE JO BROS ONLINE

The Jonas Brothers are always on the move. With albums, touring, and shooting schedules for their television show, there's no telling where they'll be next or what they'll be doing! So if you want to keep up with these supercute, superbusy brothers, here is a list of websites for ongoing updates on the Jonas Brothers!

The Jonas Brothers would want you to always be careful online. Never give out any sort of personal information—like your name, address, phone number, or the name of your school or sports team—and never try to meet someone in person that you met online. When you are surfing the Net, you have to remember that not everything you read there is true. Lots of people are creating websites out there, and sometimes they create false information to make their sites more exciting. In fact, that's one of the Jonas Brothers' pet peeves. They hate it when people leave comments pretending to be them online, but unfortunately it does happen, so take online information with a grain of salt. And remember, never surf the Web without your parents' permission. Can't find your favorite website? Websites come and go, so don't worry—there will be another one to replace it soon!

www.jonasbrothers.com

This is the Jonas Brothers' official site. It has updates on their projects and tours and an online shop where you can buy official JB gear!

www.youtube.com/JonasBrothersMusic

This is the official Jonas Brothers portion of YouTube. You can check out all of the brothers' music videos plus funny videos that the brothers post themselves! They post something new all the time, so check it often.

www.myspace.com/JonasBrothers

This is the Jonas Brothers' official MySpace page. The Jonas Brothers love MySpace. They check this page often for new friend requests and to leave messages for their fans. Check it out (with your parents' permission, of course) and add yourself to the Jonas Brothers' friend list!

www.jonasbrothersfan.com

This is a fan site devoted to everything Jonas Brothers. It has updates, fun facts about the boys, and lots of pictures.